SPELLING INQUIRY

*How One
Elementary
School
Caught the
Mnemonic
Plague*

Kelly Chandler

&

the Mapleton Teacher-Research Group

Foreword by Sandra Wilde

Stenhouse Publishers
York, Maine

Stenhouse Publishers, P.O. Box 360, York, Maine 03909
www.stenhouse.com

The authors have donated all royalties from the sale of this book to a fund to support teacher
research in Maine School Administrative District #1.

Credits
Page 27: "A Speller's Bill of Rights" by Sandra Wilde from *Primary Voices* 4. Copyright 1996
by the National Council of Teachers of English. Reprinted with permission.
Pages 29–31: *You Kan Red This! Spelling and Punctuation for Whole-Language Classrooms, K–6*
by Sandra Wilde. Copyright 1992 by Heinemann, a division of Reed Elsevier, Inc. Reprinted
with permission.
Page 73: *Spelling in Use: Looking Closely at Spelling in Whole-Language Classrooms* by Lester
Laminack and Katie Wood. Copyright 1996 by the National Council of Teachers of English.
Reprinted with permission.

Library of Congress Cataloging-in-Publication Data
Chandler, Kelly, 1970-
      Spelling inquiry : how one elementary school caught the mnemonic plague / Kelly
Chandler and the Mapleton Teacher-Research Group : foreword by Sandra Wilde.
          p.   cm.
      Includes bibliographical references (p.).
      1. English language—Orthography and spelling—Study and teaching (Elementary)—
United States—Case studies. 2. Mapleton Elementary School (Mapleton, Me.) I. Mapleton
Teacher-Research Group (Mapleton, Me.) II. Title.
LB1574.C4384   1999
372.63'2—dc21   99-10748
                          CIP

Cover photographs by Lorna Tobin and Martha LaPointe
Manufactured in the United States of America on acid-free paper
04 03 02 01 00 99 9 8 7 6 5 4 3 2 1

For Brenda Miller Power and Ruth Shagoury Hubbard,
for their belief in the power of teacher research
to transform schools for teachers and children

Contents

Foreword

Up in the northeast corner of Maine, a remarkable group of teachers has carried out a profoundly innovative and effective transformation of one curriculum area, spelling. Through a process of group inquiry, the teachers and other professionals of Mapleton Elementary became fascinated by spelling, exploring how to improve the ways in which they helped children learn to spell better.

As I've talked to teachers about spelling over the last several years, I've become aware of how challenging it is to make deep changes in how we help children learn to spell. Tradition has a strong pull. Also, we think spelling should be easy to teach, since it's such a minor and relatively simple part of the writing process, yet the English spelling system and the ways in which children learn it naturally are surprisingly complex.

Therefore, many good teachers with literature-based, child-centered literacy programs are no longer using spelling books but are unsure about what to do instead. They may, for instance, use the traditional list-test model, but with their own lists of words. Or they may feel that spelling can be picked up entirely through reading and writing, without any focused teaching. The challenge is to truly build on what we know about how spelling develops naturally and then take an active role in supporting that process. Since the rethinking involved is so deep, this process is not easy.

This book, *Spelling Inquiry*, is therefore tremendously exciting because it addresses not only what spelling curriculum might be like but how teachers can and should think about and change their practice. The authors, in deeply linking their two themes of classroom-based inquiry and improving spelling instruction, have provided a wonderful model not only for this particular area of curriculum but for how curriculum development in general should take place. Kelly Chandler and her coauthors show us that the journey matters as much as the destination, and that teachers need to learn just as students do, through discovery, collaboration, and active construction of their own ideas.

As we read the authors' stories of examining how children use and understand spelling, we see how important it is for teachers to operate out of a strong knowledge base as they look at children, and then build on what they see. An example: Martha LaPointe noticed from looking at her third graders' writing that they had trouble knowing how to spell the /k/ sound at the end of words. She drew on her own knowledge that there are three major possible spellings: *ck*, "just *k*," and *k*-silent *e*, and that the preceding vowel's spelling and sound (i.e., long or short) determine which spelling of /k/ to use. Martha then invited the students to sort thirty word cards by pattern and then come up with their own rules. How different this was from just covering spellings of /k/ when they come up in a textbook, or from never drawing children's attention to this or other spelling patterns!

It's also valuable to see how teachers can use discussion and shared reading to help each other develop more knowledge about how students' understandings work. When these teachers brainstormed all the strategies both they and their students used when trying to come up with a spelling, they realized that their options had been expanded and that a similar brainstorming process could help their students become more resourceful spellers. Through reading what others had written about spelling, particularly as a source of discussion about what they saw in their own students, the Mapleton teachers expanded their collective wisdom even more.

In *Spelling Inquiry*, we see not only the authors' thoughts and ideas but their thinking process. The book is firmly grounded in the authentic complexity of real kids and how they think, as well as in the authentic complexity of the English spelling system and how it works. Rather than trying to manage this complexity by abstracting and simplifying through uniform spelling lists and worksheets, these teachers revel in complexity, observing it, working to understand it, and basing their teaching on it.

Most of the public debates on education and "school reform" focus on methodology, programs, and standards, but seldom on what teachers should be doing other than administering programs that have been chosen for them by someone else. Yet the true future of educational change, many of us believe, lies in both teachers' and children's active, collaborative construction of knowledge. What could be more important than truly professional teachers who know what children are thinking and doing (and why), teachers whose voices then become part of the larger research community from which other teachers can learn? Brava to the talented, dedicated teachers of Mapleton Elementary School, and may they serve as a model for how curriculum change should occur.

Sandra Wilde

Acknowledgments

This book has been a truly collaborative effort, not just by the team of writers who drafted it but also by a large number of people who contributed to its production in a variety of ways. Our gratitude goes out to the following:

- Brenda Power, who first suggested that we might have a story to tell in a book, and whose own books have guided our way as teacher-researchers
- Ruth Hubbard, who has been our "distant teacher" with her writing
- Philippa Stratton, whose encouragement gave us the courage to begin and who shepherded us through the publishing process along with Tom Seavey and Martha Drury
- Mary Caron, Ann Hall, and Suzanne Stroble Kaback, who provided feedback at crucial times in our writing and thinking
- Comprehensive System for Professional Development for our 1997 grant, and the Spencer Foundation for additional funding we received through the Practitioner Communication and Mentoring Grant Program
- Matthew, Ellen, Alison, and Matt Libby at Libby's Camps (207-435-8274) for providing us with the perfect spot (and the perfect meals) for our retreat
- The staff members at Mapleton Elementary School (MES) who took care of all kinds of things so we could concentrate on our work: Bert Taylor, Sheryl Grendell, Gwen Turner, and Winnie Ireland
- Sharon O'Brien, who helped to organize the parent survey in addition to the myriad of other duties she juggles

- The educational technicians at MES who served as research partners in our classrooms: Laura Chase, Mark Kenney, Maureen Kierstead, and Carole Soucy
- Fellow M.S.A.D. #1 teachers who supported our efforts and occasionally joined us for meetings or lunch conversations about data: Len Worthley, Norma Nadeau, Paula McCrossin, Beth Ann Miller (a teacher-researcher herself), Carol Reeves, and John Reeves (who proffered his services as a retreat helper for six credits—we declined)
- Elaine Hendrickson, a seventh-grade language arts teacher at Skyway Middle School (the next stop for Mapleton students), who joined our group and provided us with a wider perspective on spelling development
- Our MES colleagues Athena Hallowell and Lyn Edgecomb, who joined us when this work was already in progress and asked many important questions that pushed our thinking
- Dr. Gehrig Johnson, M.S.A.D.#1 superintendent, and Pamela Hallett, M.S.A.D.#1 curriculum coordinator, whose support allows us to do this important work
- The students at MES and their parents, who are our most important co-researchers and the reason we pursue our inquiry
- Our families, whose support, love, and patience permit us to grow as teachers and learners

Introduction

Welcome to *Spelling Inquiry: How One Elementary School Caught the Mnemonic Plague!* Before you begin reading, it may be helpful to have a brief history about the team of teachers behind this project, as well as a road map of the chapters that follow. Although the primary focus of the book is on improving spelling instruction, it also has a strong emphasis on classroom-based inquiry. For us, it has been almost impossible to separate the two topics. While we realize that you may have chosen this book for only one of those reasons, we hope that you will find useful strategies and suggestions regarding both areas. Perhaps you'll finish reading with a new interest either in becoming a teacher-researcher or in investigating spelling more closely than you have in the past.

Now, on to the history. In December 1996, we founded a teacher-research group at Mapleton Elementary, a K–5 school in northern Maine that enrolls about 240 students. Three teachers—Martha LaPointe, Lois Pangburn, and Lynne Brabant—wrote a grant to support our work and invited Kelly Chandler, then a doctoral student at the University of Maine, to join the group as its informal facilitator. During our first year together, our focus was on reading instruction, particularly for students who struggle. All of the full-time teachers in the school and an educational technician participated on a voluntary basis. We met monthly to develop inquiry questions, share and analyze data we collected in our classrooms, and discuss professional literature on both literacy and teacher research.

During the next school year, after we had gained confidence as researchers, we were ready to tackle a topic that had been a source of tension for all of us: spelling. Our exploration lasted throughout the 1997–1998

1

school year and into the next, resulting in the writing of this book. In Chapter 1, we discuss more thoroughly the different factors that led us to conduct this whole-school inquiry.

Because spelling instruction was an area of weakness for us as a staff, it was important for us to develop a common language for our discussions and a common "gene pool" of knowledge. To this end, we collected and analyzed a variety of data, such as student writing samples and surveys, on a schoolwide basis. We also engaged in a series of activities, including the reading and discussion of professional resources, to establish what we believed about spelling and how it can best be taught. What we learned from inquiring with each other in these ways is the subject of Chapter 2.

For us, one of the most exciting aspects of this project was how our students became invested in it along with us. Chapter 3 focuses on the ways that group members involved students in their inquiries about spelling. It emphasizes the importance of exploratory talk and observational data, particularly in understanding how students help each other spell, write, and read. Just as important, it explores how teachers' interventions can nudge students' understanding forward.

In addition to collecting data directly in our classrooms, we enlisted our students' parents as informants. We'll tell you in Chapter 4 how we designed a spelling survey for parents, as well as what we learned from the data the surveys generated. We'll also discuss what we have done, and plan to do, with this information, as it has changed the way we communicate with the community about our spelling program.

Chapter 5 discusses how our assessment and evaluation of spelling improved along with our inquiry. It provides examples from all of our classrooms of how observations, conferencing, and product analysis yielded rich data about what students knew and could do as spellers, as well as pointed the way for shifts we needed to make in our practice. The chapter closes with a description of how we developed a spelling rubric that could serve as a schoolwide supplement to our report card.

The book closes with an explanation of why we see spelling as a particularly appropriate topic for classroom-based inquiry, as well as a description of how our research group works (Chapter 6). Three members of the group are profiled, and the specific roles played by several others are discussed. Finally, we propose ways that you might get started with spelling inquiries of your own and include members' tips for beginning teacher-researchers, either as individuals or as members of a research community.

Since this book was written in an unusual way, it may be useful to you to know something about the process behind it. In the summer of 1998, eleven of the group's thirteen members went on a weeklong writing and data-analysis retreat at a wilderness lodge. When we arrived at camp, we brainstormed a long list—three full chart pages!—of topics, issues, and questions that we felt should be included in this book. Kelly clustered these ideas and created a six-chapter outline from them. Then, during the rest of the week, group members chose different sections of the book to write about, either by themselves or with another person. We also wrote a ten-minute freewrite each day on topics such as "What have been your most lasting learnings about spelling?" and "What advice would you give to other teacher researchers wanting to form a group?" The writing from this week became the raw material for this book.

In the months that followed the retreat, members of the group played different roles. Some of us wrote specific sections that had not been previously addressed. On a number of occasions, small groups gathered to work on particular chapters, with a notetaker recording their conversations. Other members read drafts in progress, making comments and filling in gaps. Although Kelly took on most of the responsibility of organizing and writing transitions between sections, all of our voices can be heard throughout the text. In some sections, three or four people have had a hand in writing what appears to be a fairly seamless (we hope!) narrative.

Since our writing has been just as collaborative as our research process, we have chosen to use a collective "we" as our primary writing voice, and to refer to members within the text by their first names. Individual teachers' voices can be heard in the essays that serve as interludes between chapters, as well as in excerpts from their writing within the main text. Also sprinkled throughout the chapters are tips and strategies for both spelling instruction and classroom-based inquiry. Students' names have been changed to protect their privacy.

This project has been intellectually energizing for all of us. We hope that you will also "catch the mnemonic plague" when you read this book, and that the idea of classroom-based research on spelling will become as fascinating to you as it has been to us.

The Mapleton Teacher-Research Group
Diane Smith, kindergarten
Lynne Brabant, grade 1
Lois Pangburn, grade 1
Enola Boyce, grade 2

Judy Kenney, grade 2
Jill Brown, grade 3
Martha LaPointe, grade 3
Lorna Tobin, grade 4
Kimberley Wright, grade 4
Victoria Morrison, instructional aide
Peggy Gudreau, resource room
Gail Gibson, principal/grade 5
Kelly Chandler, facilitator

Stones in Our Shoes: How We Came to Study Spelling

Teacher research often starts with a tension, an unnamed "something" that rubs against our teaching life like a pebble in a shoe.

RUTH HUBBARD

Most teachers need look no further than spelling to find a topic that rubs against their teaching life, causing small tensions. But at Mapleton Elementary School, it took us a long time to recognize that we could do anything about this stone in our shoe.

For years, we avoided discussing spelling much. We didn't know how to talk about spelling instruction in a way that reflected our progressive philosophy of teaching yet still honored students' and parents' more traditional views of what spelling instruction should be. It wasn't such a big stone, after all, and over time we just got used to the minor discomfort we felt about this area of our teaching. When we began meeting as a teacher-research group, we probably would have nodded in agreement with those who see spelling as a "trivial problem relating to the mastery of particular conventions, more the table manners of writing than the meal itself" (Hughes and Searle 1997, 9).

Yet it was not an insignificant thing that students who came from other schools were better spellers than those who had been at Mapleton since kindergarten. In our district, we are the only one of five elementary schools to move to literature-based instruction on a schoolwide basis. Because our classrooms look and feel different from many of our counterparts' in the district, we need to be able to articulate very clearly why we teach the way we do. We also need to be able to demonstrate in ways that make sense in our community that our methods lead to results.

Although our students' performance in reading and writing on a statewide test for fourth graders has consistently been exceptional, exceeding both our comparison bands and the district average, their spelling scores on the Comprehensive Test of Basic Skills were far less impressive. Even more troubling to us was our concern that students seemed to have very little interest in spelling correctly unless a piece was to be taken completely through the writing process. For them, our message that spelling need not hamper first-draft, exploratory writing had been translated into "Spelling only matters in a few isolated situations: for example, on tests, or in your published, final drafts."

Not only did this issue present potential problems for us among other educators in the district, but we were also worried about how students' poor spelling represented our work, and theirs, to the community. Since many people associate misspellings with carelessness, laziness, and sloppiness, parents often have legitimate concerns about their children learning to spell conventionally. A prevalence of errors in our students' work could signal to parents that we didn't share those concerns, and this miscommunication might jeopardize their support of the changes we had made in our practice over the past ten years. As Gail, the school's principal and fifth-grade language arts teacher, points out,

> Poor spelling is such a visible thing. You can see it easily, like tracks in the snow. People who spell well find their eyes automatically drawn to errors, and they blame the schools. Those errors are evidence that teachers aren't doing a good job. Many parents seem to assume that a culture of permissiveness exists in classrooms that have moved toward holistic teaching. They seem to think that teachers just let kids do whatever they want.

Since our approach to literacy learning is very different from what most parents experienced when they were in school, we needed to reassure them that basic skills such as spelling were still being addressed. To keep parents' support for our literacy program from being eroded, it was crucial to help our students become more conventional spellers, as well as to encourage their development of what Richard Gentry (1997) calls "spelling consciousness": "a habit of caring about expert spelling when spelling is important" (48).

When the research group was founded, all of us were in accord on most aspects of language arts instruction. Over the last decade, we had spent a lot of time learning about literacy, beginning with a six-credit course taught on our school site entitled "Reading and Writing Process." As part of that class, everyone did a case study of a child's literacy learning, an experience that Martha, a third-grade teacher, recalls as vital in helping people to make the connection between student-centered theory and practice: "That's where it all came together. And I remember how excited we were at how smart those children were, even though many of us chose 'struggling' students to focus on." Although we didn't have a name for it then, we realize in retrospect that these case studies represented our start as teacher researchers. We were learning to teach from systematic observations of our students, and the children's work showed us what we needed to do next.

Over the years, our whole-school staff development initiatives continued, often with the assistance of small grants. Reading and discussing the work of Donald Graves (1983), Ken Goodman (1986), Lucy Calkins (1983, 1986), and Margaret Mooney (1988, 1990) reinforced and extended our thinking. We visited other schools with exemplary literacy programs, wrote grants for professional resources and tradebooks, and presented our emerging understandings at local and state conferences. One summer, we even hosted a publisher's institute on holistic language arts teaching for colleagues from the surrounding area. These common experiences helped us come to consensus on some key aspects of literacy learning that continue to undergird our practice:

- Children become better readers and writers by reading and writing as members of the "literacy club," people who are able to use written language for their own purposes (Smith 1985).
- Reading, writing, speaking, and listening are interrelated processes.
- Authentic children's literature, as opposed to basal "textoids," should be used for reading instruction; children should write about things they care about, not about contrived prompts (Smith, Carey, and Harste 1982).
- Skills should be taught in the context of whole and meaningful literacy activities.
- Teachers should build on children's strengths, rather than work from their deficits.

Although only six of the twelve teachers from the original group that took the 1986 course remained at our school, newcomers to our staff made a

T I P

Getting the Most Out of a Small Grant

1. Order professional books, particularly those written by other teacher researchers, to read and share. Publishers such as Stenhouse (www.stenhouse.com), Heinemann (www.heinemann.com), and the National Council of Teachers of English (www.ncte.org) offer inexpensive resources that can push people's thinking and spark questions for further inquiry.

2. Buy tools of the trade such as Post-its, tape flags, project planners (spiral-bound pads with a space for commenting on your notes), and two-color pens. These small, inexpensive treats help teacher-researchers get in the habit of collecting, coding, and analyzing their data.

3. Allocate some money for refreshments. Since people come to meetings more often when food is served, it's a necessity, not a foolish expense.

4. If you can spare it, build in some money for release time so that research partners can meet. If you hire two roving substitutes for a full day, two research teams can meet for about three hours apiece. This uninterrupted time to talk and analyze data can make a huge difference in people's commitment to their projects.

5. If you're interested in having an outside facilitator, hire a graduate student rather than a professional consultant or a university faculty member. The fee will be less, and it's possible that the person may have more time to devote to your project.

conscious decision to teach at Mapleton because they shared a commitment to a student-centered philosophy. As we revisited our common principles each year, these new colleagues pushed our thinking forward with fresh ideas. At the same time they validated the work we'd done before.

Spelling, unfortunately, was where our belief system broke down. We didn't offer students a consistent program as they moved from grade to grade, nor, for the most part, was our spelling instruction consistent with the tenets about literacy learning that drove the rest of our daily work with kids. Some of us continued to use a commercial program—complete with worksheets, lists, and tests—despite its lack of alignment with our reading and writing instruction. Others provided almost no explicit instruction in spelling, preferring to let students come to their knowledge of the spelling system in a "natural" way, through immersion in reading and writing tasks. A couple of members allowed students to choose their own words to study for tests, but they were often frustrated by the kids' seemingly arbitrary selections, as well as the lack of transfer to their writing. The one thing we all agreed on was that none of these approaches was working as well as we wanted.

It's doubtful, however, that any of us would have tried to extract the spelling stone from our shoe any time soon if it hadn't been for Enola. An experienced primary educator, she had taken three years off from teaching before being hired at Mapleton as a long-term substitute in third grade. Eager for conversation with colleagues, she joined the research group immediately. When we began to use our meeting time to discuss individual members' inquiries and to brainstorm research plans, Enola framed the following question: "What activities encourage students to become good spellers?" It was the only individual question that didn't deal with reading.

Enola's decision to pursue a different study from the rest of us was rooted in the discrepancy between her experience as a learner and her observations as a teacher. As it did for many teachers, spelling came easily for Enola in school. "I was the spelling champ in my eighth-grade class," she writes. "I could remember rules. I could break a word down into syllables. I could visualize it in my head. I could even picture some place where I'd seen the word. I wondered what was so difficult about all that." But if spelling was so easy, then why did many of her students struggle with the same things that seemed effortless to her? And why did her friend Elaine, who taught middle school language arts, continue to be frustrated with her students' errors? These questions nagged at Enola, and she hoped that her research would help her figure out how to close the gap, for good, between her own positive experiences and her students' difficulties:

> I was concerned that I was not doing something right in my teaching of spelling. And if spelling was still a problem in seventh grade, then what was happening between early elementary and middle school? Were teachers failing? Was it the program, the system? What was going on here? I was looking for a sure-fix, an easy way to teach spelling to my students. I was positive there had to be an answer to my question.

At the end of our first year of research, Enola's answer was still absent, but her inquiry had engaged the rest of us in the group more than any other individual question. Her work also brought to the surface the staff's discomfort about spelling. Gail explains it this way: "Because Enola's question kept coming up again and again in our meetings, we had to face something that we all felt but hadn't voiced: that we weren't providing consistent instruction in spelling—and that we weren't really integrating it with the writing process, even though we said we were."

When it came time for the group to select an umbrella topic for our second year of research, we decided to begin with spelling. "Maybe we'll get somewhere if we *all* work on Enola's question," Kelly, our facilitator, joked at a meeting. At that point, we all decided to take off our shoes and risk going barefoot while we removed the spelling stone for further examination. It wasn't easy, however, to make this decision. The following transcript excerpt from our first research-group meeting of 1997–98 demonstrates the degree of uncertainty felt by many members about this area of their teaching, as well as the degree of urgency we had come to feel about the need to change things:

September 23, 1997
The group has unanimously decided to pursue spelling as our group topic, but we have not decided what to do next. Nancy Andrews, a consultant with the state department of education, is visiting on this day.

KELLY: So how do you think we should proceed? How would you like to go about this inquiry?

MARTHA: I don't know, but I think this is important. The kids are getting different approaches, and that's not fair to them. Kids from other schools are better spellers when they come to us, although they're not better readers and writers. I want us to be the best at everything. [*Laughs.*] I'm really anxious to get started.

NANCY: You've already got some of your kids trained as observers [*referring to the notetaking many students did during our first year as a research group*].

GAIL: Spelling is the area we're most inconsistent in. We don't know what each other is doing.

LORNA: I don't even know what I'm doing!

MARTHA: I want to know why I'm doing it.

ENOLA: What should I be doing?

JILL: Can you even teach kids to spell well?

GAIL [*dryly*]: Obviously somebody's doing it well.

NANCY: Maybe only good spellers transfer. [*Everybody laughs.*]

T I P

> ### Your First Inquiry-Group Meeting
>
> - Choose a location that most teachers will pass: the teachers' lounge, the cafeteria if it's on the way to the parking lot, a room near the office.
> - Set the date well in advance so people can arrange for rides, child-care, etc. Then remind people with a poster or an e-mail message a day or two before the meeting.
> - Schedule the meeting as a continuation of another one that's required. Gail often compresses our faculty-meeting agenda so there will be contractually guaranteed time left for research-group talk.
> - Set a definite ending time so people know how much time they need to commit. End early, rather than late, and some folks may come back to continue an unfinished conversation.
> - Order pizza—food's a great draw, and the smell may attract people who will decide to stay.
> - Don't limit your invitees to full-time, on-site faculty; welcome instructional aides, student interns, and itinerant teachers.
> - Appoint a facilitator with enough influence to nudge the group beyond negativity if the discussion edges there.
> - Leave your charts up or post your minutes in a public place to intrigue those who missed the session—maybe they'll be curious enough to join you next time.

Just because we knew our spelling research would benefit us and our students didn't necessarily mean we were overjoyed about undertaking it. In fact, we began our work together with a take-your-medicine kind of mind-set that did not resemble the excitement we felt during our reading inquiry the year before. We planned to tackle the spelling problem with as much collective energy as we could muster . . . and then to move on to something more interesting once we had things figured out. Yet this isn't what happened at all.

We knew that we were hooked on our topic the day we spent part of a research-group meeting generating a list of strategies we used as adult spellers (see Chapter 2 for a more complete description of this process). After "make sure each syllable has a vowel" and "substitute letters you know make the same sound" were added to the list, Gail offered another suggestion: "Put down that you can use mnemonic devices. You know, like 'a friend is a friend till the *-end*' or 'the principal is your *pal*.'"

As Kelly wrote this contribution on chart paper, Martha peered at the word *mnemonic* with puzzlement and said, "Is that really how that's spelled? I don't think so." While Enola went off to her classroom to get a dictionary, the rest of us "had a go," trying to write the word several ways to see what looked right. There were both squeals of delight and groans of disappointment among group members when the original spelling was revealed to be correct. Then all of us chuckled about how caught up in this minor spelling challenge we had become. As we refocused our attention on the list of strategies we were generating, Kelly pointed to the chart and exclaimed, "Guess we just caught the mnemonic plague!" The meeting dissolved in laughter again, and it was a while before we managed to return to work. Both the pun and the group's digression to spell the word helped us to realize how much fun our inquiry could be.

When we began, between scheduled meetings, to observe student writers at work, we realized that spelling is a far more complex process than we had assumed—and therefore far more interesting to explore as teacher researchers. The more we read and talked as a group, the richer our classroom observations were, and the more sophisticated our thinking became. It was an important first step for us to make a list of strategies for spelling an unknown word. But our conversations moved to another level when we began to consider the broader contexts in which these strategies might be used. Every day in writers' workshop, students might be making any one (or more) of dozens of spelling-related decisions:

- How much time should I spend spelling this word? Am I going to get distracted from the flow of my writing if I stop?
- Do I need to invent a spelling for this word, or is it a "one-second word" (Wilde 1997) that I could get right if I thought about it briefly?
- Am I going to need this word throughout my piece? Is it worth taking the time to get it right now, rather than having to do a lot of editing later?
- Have I ever seen this word in print before? If so, where? What other words might look like it?
- Should I try the word a couple of different ways, write the first letter followed by a dash, or look for it in a resource in the room?

We realized that determining the most efficient strategy for spelling a word required students to draw on knowledge from reading, to be aware of their surroundings, to use analogies, and to know themselves as writers.

Most of the time, the decision-making process was implicit, under the surface of students' minds rather than consciously reasoned, but that did not make it any less complex. And we also realized that the more often we could open up that process to students—to demonstrate how we made decisions ourselves as writers, to help them reflect on what worked and didn't work—the more flexible, efficient, and purposeful the children could be in their spelling. Had we ever seen a spelling textbook that addressed these issues at length? We weren't familiar with one.

It has become common in our profession to hear teachers talking about the need for students to construct their own understandings of concepts and ideas (Wood 1988; Brooks and Brooks 1993; Short, Harste, and Burke 1996). Many people advocate for learning environments that engage kids in looking for patterns, testing hypotheses, and formulating conclusions. According to Stephanie Harvey (1998), such inquiry-based teaching allows students "to understand what they learn, rather than merely retell it. This

---

T ▶ I ▶ P

Modeling Your Spelling Process

1. Use an overhead projector, not the chalkboard, so your body won't block students' view of your writing.

2. Provide a running commentary about your decision making as you write (e.g., "I know I always have a hard time spelling this word, *gauge,* so I'll take an extra second to see if it looks right").

3. Model your spelling within the context of writing a short piece, not simply spelling a list of words. This way, students will see how you balance attention to spelling with other writerly concerns.

4. Write on a topic that will make it easier to include some words that are genuinely challenging for you to spell. Kids will mistrust the model if you're not genuine; they know you can spell *cat* without much thought!

5. Demonstrate how you construct a placeholder spelling (e.g., "I'm going to include the sounds I hear and go on"), as well as how you mark it to be sure to check it later (e.g., "I think I'll circle this so I won't miss it when I do my final edit").

6. Model the use of multiple strategies, as well as cross-checking (e.g., "I've tried this word several different ways—this one looks right to me, and it's spelled like another word I know with the same sound in the middle, but I think I'll check it in the dictionary to make sure").

understanding leads to insight, which occurs in kindergartners as well as Ph.D. candidates. Insight leads to new questions not possible before" (2).

We have become convinced that teachers need the same opportunities for insight as many young learners. Although teachers frequently facilitate the inquiry process for the children in their classrooms, they do not always have a lot of experience with this same process around their own teaching. In this case, it's easy to look to someone else to provide the answers. Here's a notable example: When we told some colleagues from another school about our retreat plans, one woman responded, "Great! I can't wait till you get back so you can tell us what to do!"

We know what it's like to feel this way—to wish that Some Expert would provide the answers in clear, simple terms. Many of us have shelves full of professional books on spelling that we bought hoping someone had written the perfect blueprint for our classroom practice. Like Enola, everyone wanted a "sure-fix." Only now, after nearly a year's worth of work on the topic, do we feel confident about trusting our own judgment rather than an outsider's. We hope this book will help you develop the same kind of confidence in your own practice.

We believe that one of the reasons spelling became such a stone in our shoes was that our teacher education programs and our subsequent staff development provided few chances for us to construct our own understandings about spelling. We had read or heard about things like developmental spelling stages, word walls, and personal dictionaries, but these were bits of received knowledge about teaching spelling. They came directly from other people's insights, not our own, and we struggled to integrate them and make sense of them within the contexts of our own classrooms. Only when we began to plumb the data from our own teaching, talking through their implications with each other and our students, did we begin to understand the spelling process in a deep way.

In keeping with this important insight about our own learning, we pose more questions than we provide answers in the following pages. We do not claim to be experts on teaching spelling, and we hope that readers will engage in critical dialogue with us throughout the book—weighing our stories against what they have seen and heard themselves. This is not a "how to" book, though we do believe it is a practical one and one that is rooted in the everyday experiences of real teachers and real kids. We hope that you will find lessons in it that are immediately useful to you, that you will hear your own voice in a quote from a group member or perhaps see one of your own students in a vignette of a classroom activity. At the same time, we

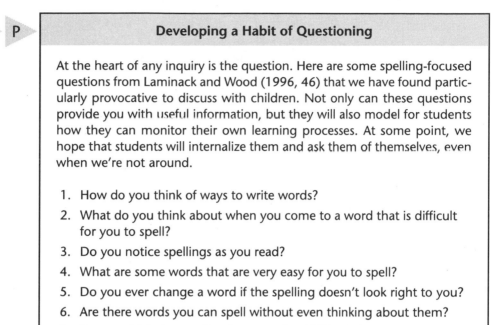

Developing a Habit of Questioning

At the heart of any inquiry is the question. Here are some spelling-focused questions from Laminack and Wood (1996, 46) that we have found particularly provocative to discuss with children. Not only can these questions provide you with useful information, but they will also model for students how they can monitor their own learning processes. At some point, we hope that students will internalize them and ask them of themselves, even when we're not around.

1. How do you think of ways to write words?
2. What do you think about when you come to a word that is difficult for you to spell?
3. Do you notice spellings as you read?
4. What are some words that are very easy for you to spell?
5. Do you ever change a word if the spelling doesn't look right to you?
6. Are there words you can spell without even thinking about them?
7. Do you think that spelling is easy or hard? Why?

want to help you take action, to think vigorously about how *you* might engage in similar kinds of inquiry with other teachers, with your students, and with community members, like we did.

For this reason, you will find Extensions at the end of each chapter that are designed to help you explore some of the issues raised throughout the book. Many of the suggestions will require you to collect data of some kind, or to try out a particular idea with your students. Some are particularly appropriate for teachers to pursue with other colleagues, and we hope that you will be able to enlist a partner or perhaps to gather a small group as you work through those options. (Our commitment to this kind of collaborative inquiry is discussed in more detail in the following chapter.) Nonetheless, we firmly believe that any individual teacher can learn from these activities, particularly if he or she is willing to engage students and/or parents as co-researchers.

Extensions

1. Reflect on your own spelling history. Make a list of memories related to spelling, and think about their implications for your teaching, as Enola

did. What factors have affected the way you feel about spelling, both as a teacher and a writer?

2. Gather some information about how spelling is taught across grade levels in your school. If you do not have a concrete or complete sense of how your colleagues are approaching spelling instruction, you might want to develop and distribute a brief survey. You might also call a before-school or lunch meeting to share information about individuals' goals and procedures for teaching spelling.

3. Talk to people outside your faculty regarding spelling. How do community members who aren't teachers talk about spelling? How do their perceptions and attitudes compare to your own and those of your colleagues? You may want to use some of the following questions to structure brief, informal interviews:

- What words or phrases do you associate with the term "good speller"? With the term "poor speller"?
- How do you think people become good spellers?
- What kinds of expectations exist in your workplace for correct spelling?
- What kinds of strategies do you use as a speller?

INTERLUDE

Investigating Spelling Patterns Through the Daily Newsletter

LOIS PANGBURN, GRADE 1

May 26, 1998

Rebecca, Patrick, and Shawn are working together to compile the newsletter that will be read by the whole class later in the morning. I am sitting nearby in a student chair, taking notes. Rebecca is looking at Patrick's word, *Mothers.*

REBECCA: You need a comma in there. You need a comma in there. You need a comma in there. [*Patrick adds an apostrophe in the right spot and writes the word* house. *Rebecca comments on his* H.]

REBECCA: That's an A with a scribble at the top of it!

PATRICK: Sooorry!
REBECCA: I'm trying to help you!
PATRICK: Then you write it. . . . No, I want to write it!
MRS. PANGBURN: You mean correct spelling?
PATRICK [*whining*]: Yes!
MRS. PANGBURN: What can you do to find out?

Patrick's eyes scan the room. He is the king of environmental print. Shawn leaves the group and is back in a flash with a picture dictionary. All three children cluster around the book on the floor. They find the *H* section. They find the words *home* and *house*, discuss the differences, and identify the one that Patrick should use. They then go back to their work.

My feet are practically touching the book—I am that close to them. No one asks me for my opinion.

Each September, I used to introduce a daily newsletter as part of our morning routine in first grade. I viewed the newsletter as an authentic reading opportunity. It was a place to teach letters, sounds, spacing, and left-to-right progression in a meaningful context, as well as a way to communicate to the children what they could expect in our day together. I wrote the letter each morning, using careful penmanship because I wanted even the script to represent good models for the children.

Last year was no different than previous years—at least at first. Within a few weeks of establishing this daily routine, several children hurried to be first to gather around the newsletter each morning and work to decipher as much of the information as possible before the group reading planned for later. They wanted to know what was going to be happening that day. It reminded me of adults needing to read the paper in the morning or teachers touching base in the teachers' room to stay current with school news. The newsletter was a link, connecting kids to a literate life, and I was completely in control of it. The power was heady.

So, how did this particular group of children wrest control of my beloved newsletter away from me? As in so many stories told in retrospect, I can see now that it happened by degrees. When you're a teacher-researcher you have little question marks in your head all the time. They are at the end of questions like:

Is this kid-centered?
Is this doing what I want it to do?

How can I make this better?
What needs to happen next?

Since I had all of these questions in my head anyway, it was only natural that they got louder when the K–5 teacher-research group decided to
investigate spelling in our building. I decided to make it a point each day to
consider a new word taken from the newsletter. I called it "pulling a word
out." After we had worked our way through the reading of the newsletter,
one child would volunteer to identify a word to be pulled out. Any word was
okay. Another child would determine what we'd "do" with it. We would circle the word in the newsletter, and then we'd begin our investigation, such
as finding other words that rhyme, at the bottom of the sheet. I never knew
for sure where we were going, but we always ended up in an interesting
place (see Figure 1.1 from February 26, 1998). We covered a lot. We found
double *o*s tucked in the middle of words like *toot*, *boot*, and *flood*. We discovered as a group that there were predictable patterns in words like *tar*, *far*,
and *star*, but that there were renegade words, too, like *are*, that insisted on
going their own way.

The newsletter had gotten much shorter by now since we needed room
at the bottom for our word investigations. We began saving the newsletters
and kept them hanging in a corner so kids could go back into them—sometimes to find a spelling they needed, sometimes to add a find. I loved the day
that quiet Jacques interjected that the word *corral*, which we were adding to
the *c* list, could also go on the "double *r*" list. I handed him my pen and he
wrote it there.

The children were becoming more involved, but there was something
else bothering me. How could I make this better? I had a purpose in my
head for this word pulling. I wanted this activity to raise children's awareness of spelling patterns and, in doing so, to generate usable word lists for
reference. The children were content listing words with the same beginning
letters or words that rhymed. While both of these explorations were legitimate and useful, I wanted them to expand their vision of discovery. I
wanted to get to other possibilities while still following their lead. So we
began to brainstorm *several* directions in which we could go with the word
each day, and I would pick one of those directions from the list. By March,
the listing had taken on a new flavor (see Figure 1.2 from March 25, 1998).

Something else happened to the newsletter in late March. I'd been
introduced to interactive writing—a technique in which students share the
teacher's pen one at a time, to compose a whole-group message—in a writ-

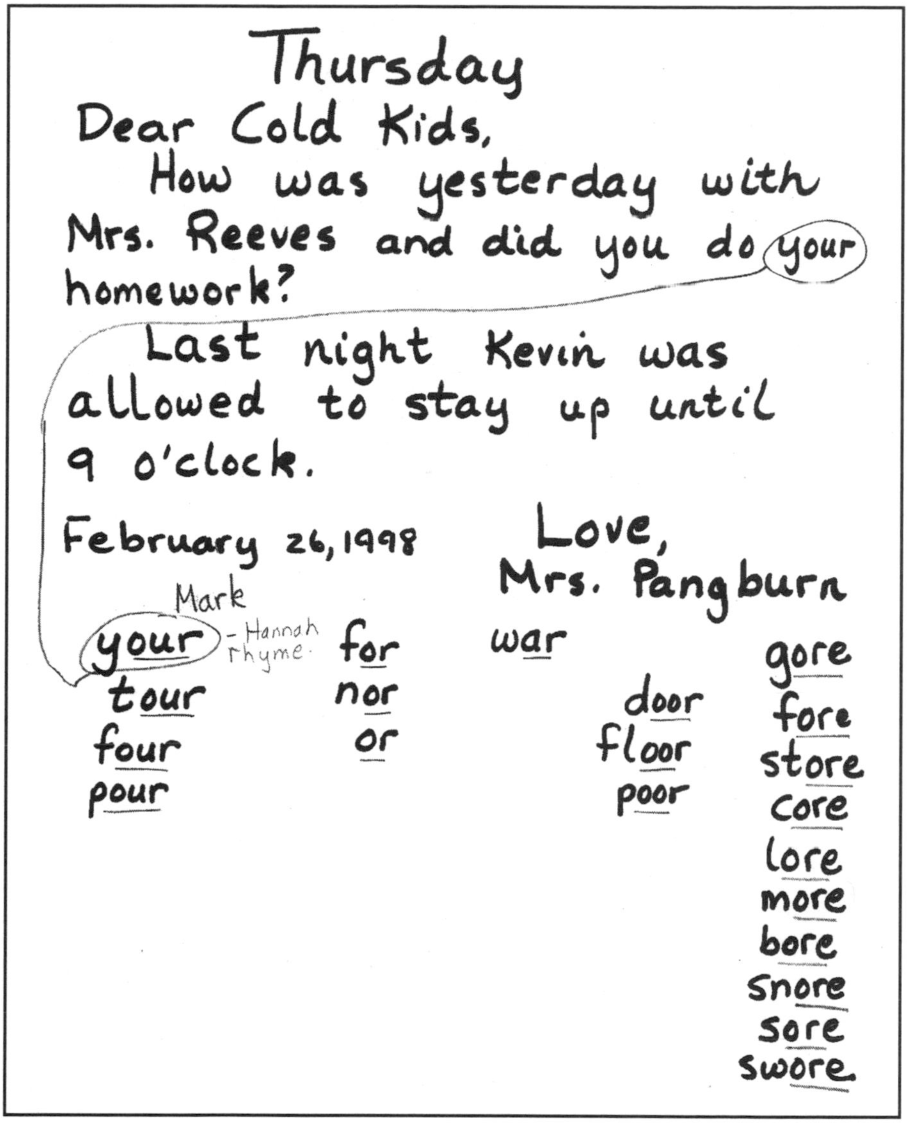

Thursday

Dear Cold Kids,

How was yesterday with Mrs. Reeves and did you do (your) homework?

Last night Kevin was allowed to stay up until 9 o'clock.

February 26, 1998

Mark

(your) - Hannah
rhyme.
tour
four
pour

for
nor
or

Love,
Mrs. Pangburn

war

door
floor
poor

gore
fore
store
core
lore
more
bore
snore
sore
swore

Figure 1.1 February 26 morning message from Lois Pangburn's classroom

ing course I'd taken one summer with Dr. Rosemary Bamford at the University of Maine. Apparently I hadn't been "developmentally ready" to embrace it at the time. Was it a control issue, a time factor, a blind spot? I'm not sure, but when I saw a second demonstration in another course I was convinced that this was, indeed, too powerful to ignore. Children were constructing knowledge about spelling on the spot. I was trying to follow my

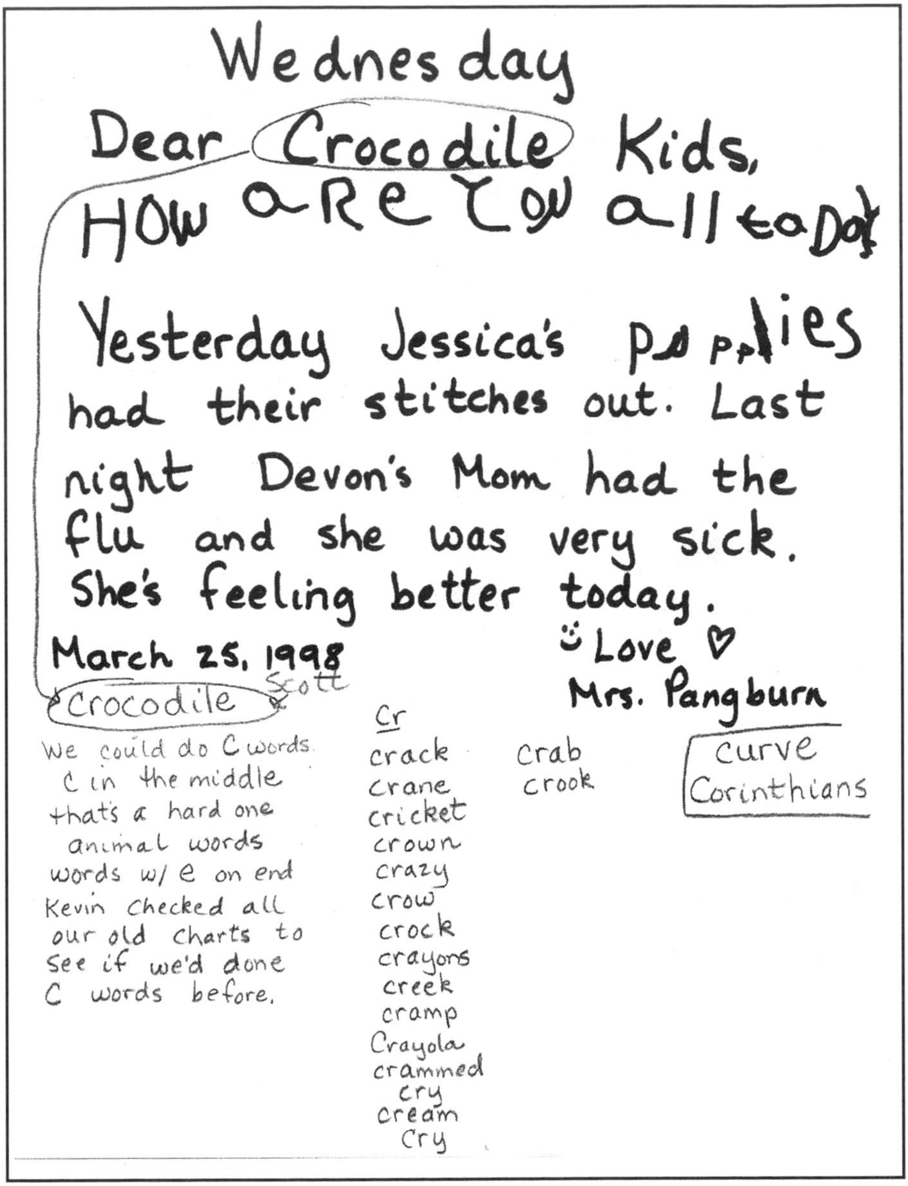

We dnes day
Dear (Crocodile) Kids,
HOW aRe You all toDay

Yesterday Jessica's popplies had their stitches out. Last night Devon's Mom had the flu and she was very sick. She's feeling better today.

March 25, 1998   ☺Love ♡
(Crocodile) Scott   Mrs. Pangburn

We could do C words.   Cr
C in the middle   crack   crab   (curve
that's a hard one   crane   crook   Corinthians)
 animal words   cricket
words w/ e on end   crown
Kevin checked all   crazy
our old charts to   crow
see if we'd done   crock
C words before.   crayons
                            creek
                            cramp
                            Crayola
                            crammed
                            cry
                            cream
                            Cry

Figure 1.2 March 25 morning message from Lois Pangburn's classroom

question "What needs to happen next?" and the answer was "You need to let go of the pen, Mrs. Pangburn!"

The children and I began taking turns as we composed the newsletter. In this way, we could consider things like the standard spelling for a word they were closely approximating, how to create spaces between words, or

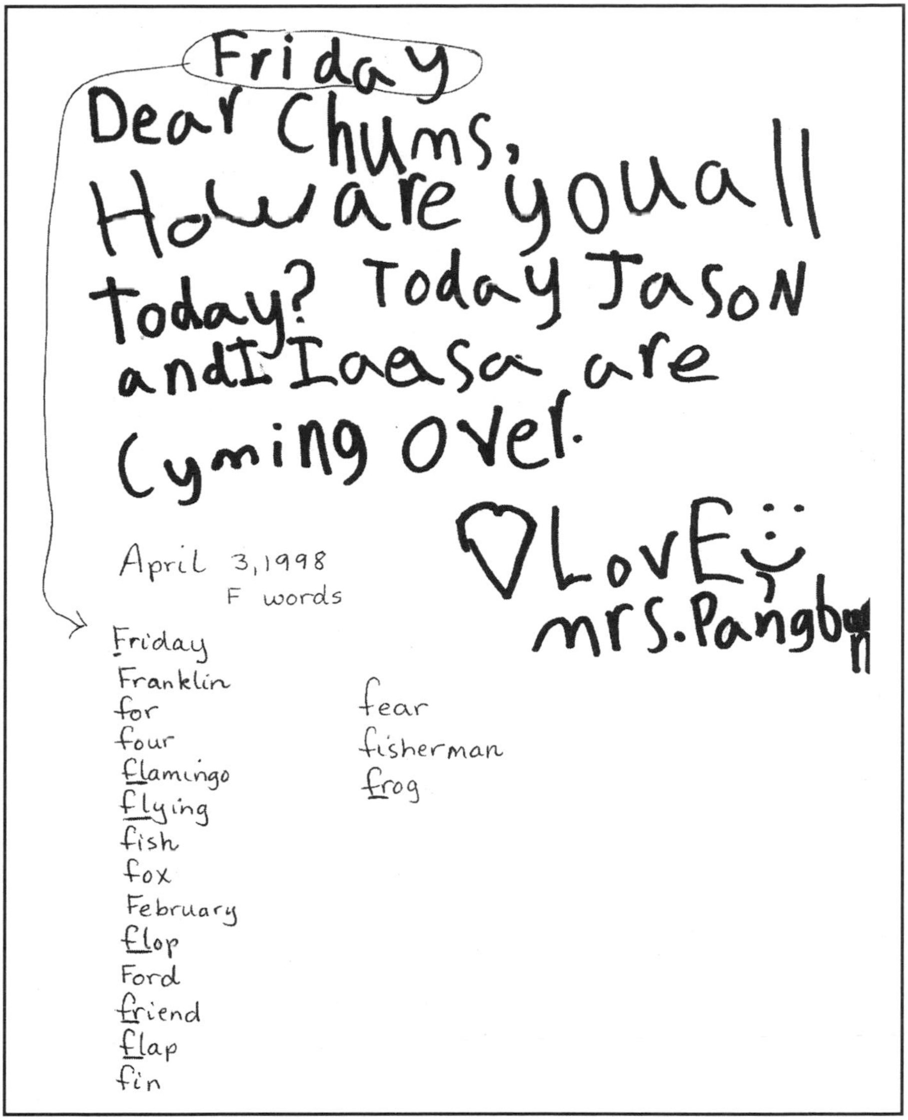
Friday
Dear Chums,
How are you all
today? Today Jason
andI Iaasa are
Cyming over.
♡ Love
mrs.Pangb

April 3, 1998
F words

Friday
Franklin
for
four
flamingo
flying
fish
fox
February
flop
Ford
friend
flap
fin
fear
fisherman
frog

Figure 1.3 April 3 morning message from Lois Pangburn's classroom

lowercase letter formation. But we were still writing "my" news. By April 3, however, the children were composing the entire letter, and my hand was seen only where I used the masking tape (we used it appropriately to "mask" errors and fix them up) and where I had recorded the date and listed the words at the bottom (see Figure 1.3, April 3, 1998). This stage in our evolution was exciting. The children were thrilled to be doing the "teacher's

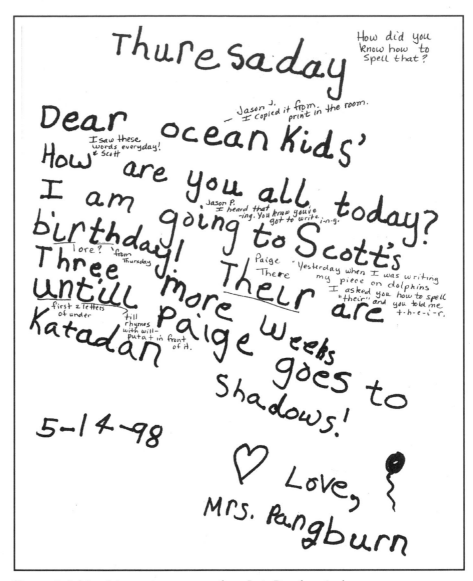

Figure 1.4 May 14 morning message from Lois Pangburn's classroom

work." They reveled in writing "their" news, and I was gaining insights into their thinking about spelling.

In mid-May I began to ask and record their answers to "How did you know how to spell that?" (see Figure 1.4, May 14, 1998). As they spoke, I scribed their information in pencil in the margin of the newsletter so I could refer to it later.

The children and I were learning a lot, but it was mid-May, we were an "active" group, and Mrs. Pangburn was getting tired. It was time to adapt. I returned to my question: "Is this doing what I want it to do?" No, it wasn't. It was taking too much time in a way that involved too few kids. Maybe some teacher in Chicago had this sharing-the-pen thing mastered, but there was a teacher in northern Maine who was moving on.

I moved the chart to the back of the room, put out Sharpies, and wrote three names on the chalkboard. I casually mentioned at the end of the day that "I would really appreciate it if these three people could please write the newsletter for us tomorrow morning." I had deliberately composed a mixed trio of writers with varied capabilities. The next day I sat down to observe and take notes as Shay, Jeff, and Paula began to write the newsletter.

SHAY: Paula, can I just explain something here? Jeff and I are going to write the date.
PAULA: Okay, but guess what? I'm writing next.
JEFF: I want to write *Saturday*.
[*Paula left and returned with a word card taken from our calendar.*]
SHAY: That's a good way to spell it!

They were empowered. They were collaborating and cooperating. But, more important, they were constructing their own understandings about reading and writing and spelling. I came into the picture as needed. Sometimes I was a resource, helping them figure out what happened to the blue picture dictionary Eileen had yesterday. Sometimes I helped resolve conflicts among the group members. Most of the time, I was just nearby, taking notes on their work.

Each time a group of students brought their finished letter back to the rest of the class, we all came together to appreciate the real work that had been done for us and to learn from and with each other. When the children saw my interest in what they were thinking, when they saw me documenting who said what right on the newsletter, they became active participants in this spelling research. They pushed themselves to look inward at their own thinking so they could articulate that information to the rest of us. As a teacher-researcher, I was reminded once again that when I have questions in my head, I should look to the children in my class.

Forget Freddie: Inquiring About Spelling with Each Other

In late June, right before we went on our teacher-research retreat, Judy, a second-grade teacher, received promotional material in her mailbox for an award-winning software package on teaching spelling. She tucked it into her folder of student data and brought it along on the retreat, where nearly all of the members of the research group were able to examine and discuss it. Hosted by a wild-haired, bright-eyed cartoon creature—we'll call him Freddie Phoneme—the program incorporated "everything children need to really succeed with spelling": graded difficulty; repetition of problem words; and games such as word searches, crossword puzzles, and flash cards. As the brochure proudly stated, "It's hard to believe that learning to spell could be so easy."

These were Enola's thoughts exactly, although she may not have been reading this sentence in the way the publisher intended! Like the rest of us, she was skeptical about whether any software, however well designed, could live up to its company's claims without support from a knowledgeable teacher. Here's a response she wrote after she and Judy previewed the program together:

We, as teachers, are the true programs of instruction. Who knows the needs of our students better than we do? We spend day after day, week after week, in classrooms full of young, ready-to-learn, ready-to-try students. Our call is to provide the opportunities, the parameters, in which these students can learn and grow. In my years of teaching, I have not inhaled the one correct way to teach spelling, nor do I expect to find such a thing. So, Freddie, I'm sorry, but you're not invited into my classroom!

In some ways, basal spelling programs make promises that are similar to Freddie's (although, admittedly, they tend to be more subtle in their promotional material). When our district was considering adopting a new series that integrated reading, language arts, and spelling, several of us attended an informational session hosted by the publisher's representative. To us, the underlying message of the session was that teachers don't need to know much about how spelling works in order to help their students become successful spellers. All they need to do is initiate and monitor a series of worry-free activities designed by expert consultants, and spelling achievement should take care of itself.

We don't mean to suggest that basal spelling programs are useless, or that there's no legitimate reason for students to practice their spelling skills using a computer program. Freddie Phoneme may indeed help some students to become more confident spellers, and our spelling series may provide some teachers with the scaffolding they need to design meaningful instruction. By the time we convened our first spelling-focused research meeting, however, most of us had serious doubts about the potential of systematic, sequenced programs to deliver what they promised. As we saw it, the writing process was too complex to be broken into components that could then be drilled to mastery. Furthermore, too many of our students (some of them diligent and conscientious ones whose parents worked hard with them at home) had faithfully done those systematic, structured activities and *still* failed to become good spellers in their writing.

These concerns left us with a quandary. If we weren't going to use a commercial program, and we were no longer comfortable with the laissez-faire approach to teaching spelling, then how were we going to structure our work with students? If we were really going to "forget Freddie" and his instructional cousins, then what were we going to do instead, and how would we decide on that course of action?

In the past, when we wanted to improve our reading instruction, we generated research questions and gathered classroom-based data to help us determine our next steps. Although group members served as resources for each other during meetings, each of us pursued a topic of her own choice. With spelling, we realized that the group needed deeper and more sophisticated knowledge before any of us could embark upon independent research journeys. We just didn't know enough about how spelling worked, or what instructional practices supported students' development, to frame good inquiry questions as individuals.

Consequently, we spent a good deal of time at the beginning of our research on spelling doing a series of activities together that was intended to increase our understanding of spelling development, as well as to gather information about our students' skills and attitudes as spellers. Only after we had this common "gene pool" of knowledge did we feel comfortable tackling our own inquiry projects, many of which are discussed in the next chapter and as Interludes and Tips throughout the rest of the text. For us, inquiring with each other provided a necessary knowledge base and a comfort zone regarding spelling that allowed us to learn more from our classroom-based explorations than we would have otherwise. We hope that the detailed descriptions of these activities in the remainder of this chapter will help you build *your* knowledge base about spelling, either on your own or in collaboration with other teachers.

The Speller's Bill of Rights

Because our spelling practices were so inconsistent, as we discussed in Chapter 1, we believed it was important to get our assumptions out in the open and discuss them before we went too far with our inquiry. A Speller's Bill of Rights, devised by Sandra Wilde (1996a, 8), served as both a starting point for our discussion and a self-evaluation tool. It was an important way for us to begin our work together, and we returned to the ideas in the document in our conversations throughout the year.

When we came together to discuss this document at our second meeting, Kelly asked everyone to choose two rights they felt they were doing a good job "protecting" for students in their classrooms, as well as two rights they felt they needed to address more squarely. In order to get a sense of where the group stood, we charted our strengths and weaknesses with pluses and minuses:

1. The right to express yourself in first-draft writing regardless of what words you do and don't know how to spell (+ + + +)
2. The right to do a lot of reading, which is probably the greatest single factor in spelling acquisition (+ + + + + +)

3. The right to actively construct knowledge about the spelling system
(- - - - - - -)
4. The right to learn that spelling does matter (+ - - - -)
5. The right to developmentally appropriate education in spelling (+ - - -)
6. The right to know about and have available a lot of ways to come up
with spellings (including just knowing how to spell the word) (++ - -)
7. The right to learn to proofread (-)
8. The right to have spelling placed in its proper context as a small piece
of the writing and language-learning process (+ + -)
9. The right to be valued as a human being regardless of your spelling (++)

When we looked at this document, some trends were clear. Across
grade levels, students at Mapleton were doing a lot of reading (#2), and they
were being encouraged to invent spellings as needed in their first-draft writing (#1). We felt that these commonalities were positive ones, providing a
good foundation from which to build the rest of our work.

More than half of our members, however, admitted with a little sheep-
ishness that they did not feel they were providing students with the opportunity to construct their own understandings of the spelling system (#3).
Although we were helping students spell words they needed to edit their
writing, for example, we weren't necessarily helping them transfer that
knowledge to similar words. Nor were we giving them enough opportunities
to think through the rules that governed spelling, as well as the places
where those rules broke down or came into conflict with each other.
Addressing this weakness in our teaching became one of our goals for the
year, and you will see as you move through later sections of this book how
several members' research projects focused on spelling activities designed to
promote these understandings.

Another concern was that students weren't necessarily getting the message that spelling does matter (#4)—and not just in pieces that are taken
through multiple drafts. A prime example that we discussed in a meeting
was Kelly's conversation with Monica, a second grader who had finished her
daily journal entry early and was waiting for her teacher to come over to her
desk and write her a response. When Kelly asked if Monica had checked her
work for spelling and punctuation, Monica gave her a pitying look and said,
"This is my *journal*—don't you get it? I don't have to do that stuff here."
While she had understood her teacher's message that journal writing was
primarily concerned with fluency and expression, she hadn't internalized
the accompanying expectation that she would self-edit her work whenever

possible to make it easier to read. Talking about this incident helped us to realize that, as a staff, we needed to help students like Monica take more responsibility for their spelling across more writing contexts.

Starting with the Speller's Bill of Rights and connecting it with examples like this one helped us keep theoretical concerns at the front of our minds while ensuring that our conversations would not get too far from students' work. It was important to us that our spelling practices stemmed from a unified set of principles consistent with our philosophy of literacy learning. We didn't want to replace the basal spelling series with a teacher-generated "bag of tricks"; instead, we hoped to develop responsive instructional plans that kept spelling in its proper place in the writing process while ensuring that all students received the assistance—direct and indirect—they needed to become conventional spellers.

Analyzing Student Surveys

Discussion of the Speller's Bill of Rights helped us begin to evaluate our teaching of spelling. A little later in the fall, when we decided to survey students about their attitudes and assumptions about spelling, we were able to check our perceptions of our teaching against student data.

In order to facilitate easy comparison of the information, we all agreed to use a set of questions adapted from Wilde (1992). Individual teachers chose to administer the survey in different ways, however, depending upon the independence level of their students and the kinds of help teachers had available to them. For example, Lynne, Lois, and Laura Chase (the instructional aide who worked with both teachers) interviewed all of the first graders individually and wrote their responses on the forms, while upper-level teachers asked their children to write their answers themselves. See Figure 2.1 for a survey that was completed by Gregory, a fifth grader.

Martha used this activity as a way to initiate a conversation with parents about how spelling was addressed in third grade (Chapter 4 includes more discussion of ways to communicate with parents). She sent a copy of the questions home on the back of a newsletter that discussed some of the trends she observed in students' responses. Here's an excerpt from the newsletter:

Another interesting student response is that spelling is based on sounds letters represent. True, to an extent, but spelling is a visual skill more

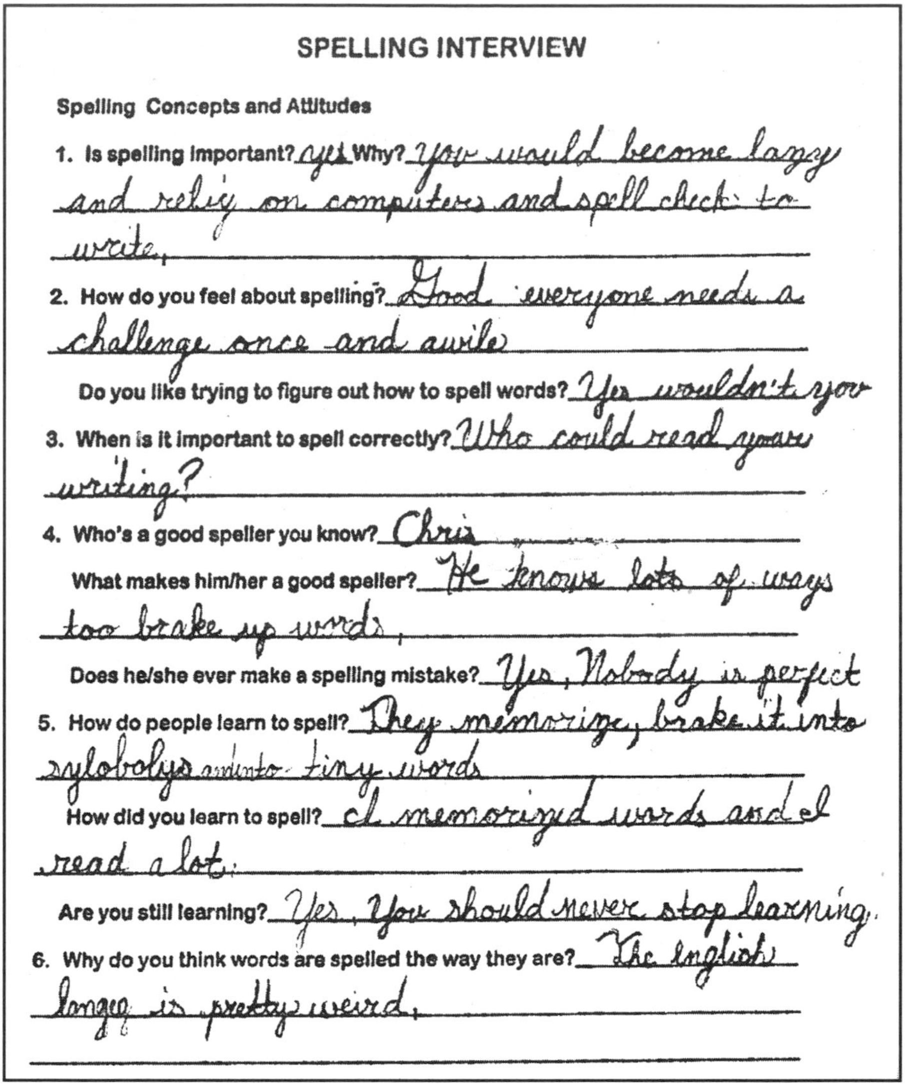

SPELLING INTERVIEW

Spelling Concepts and Attitudes

1. Is spelling important? _yes_ Why? _You would become lazy and reliy on computer and spell check to write._

2. How do you feel about spelling? _Good everyone needs a challenge once and awile_

   Do you like trying to figure out how to spell words? _Yes wouldn't you_

3. When is it important to spell correctly? _Who could read your writing?_

4. Who's a good speller you know? _Chris_

   What makes him/her a good speller? _He knows lots of ways too brake up words._

   Does he/she ever make a spelling mistake? _Yes, Nobody is perfect_

5. How do people learn to spell? _They memorize, brake it into sylobolys or into tiny words_

   How did you learn to spell? _I memorized words and I read a lot._

   Are you still learning? _Yes, You should never stop learning._

6. Why do you think words are spelled the way they are? _The english longeg is pretty weird._

Figure 2.1 Sample spelling interview completed by a student

than an auditory one. Consonant sounds are quite reliable, but it's those vowels that are the outlaws when it comes to spelling by sound. And how would you explain spelling by sound by someone from the South or downeast Maine? . . . Students have to learn to use their mind's eye to picture the words they are learning to spell. It is in this visual sense that spelling and reading are connected.

Name __Darlene_____   Date __10-3-97_____

SPELLING INTERVIEW

Spelling Concepts and Attitudes

1. Is spelling important? _yes_ Why? _If we can not spell correctly it would be difficult for others to understand what we write._

2. How do you feel about spelling? _I like to try to spell correctly._

Do you like trying to figure out unknown words? _yes_

3. When is it important to spell correctly? _Same as #1 I believe we should always try to spell correctly._

4. Who's a good speller you know? _Chris_

What makes him a good speller? _Maybe just luck, but hopefully, because he enjoys reading!_

Does he/she ever make a spelling mistake? _yes_

5. How do people learn to spell? _People learn to spell by seeing words used in sentences._

How did you learn to spell? _I learned by sounding-out the words_

Are you still learning? _yes_

6. Why do you think words are spelled the way they are? _Words are groups of letters put together. Each letter has it's own sound._

Figure 2.2 Sample spelling interview completed by a parent

When half a dozen of those parents sent back completed questionnaires, Martha received useful data about the origins of attitudes students' answers revealed. One parent's response appears in Figure 2.2.

Martha also took the lead in the group concerning data analysis. After her students completed their questionnaires, she devised a grid to collate and represent her students' responses on a single page. "That's the way I can see patterns," she explained. "I'm such a visual learner. I needed it to be all there in one spot." Since it was helpful to her, Martha decided to make her method available to the rest of the group: "I wondered if maybe others would like to use this form to assemble their data. I put a couple of copies out on the table in the teacher's room, and a sample of the one I'd done." Eventually, everyone in the research group tried out Martha's method except for Enola, who, true to her maverick form, developed a slightly different approach.

For us, these data summaries had the following advantages:

1. They forced us to think about what was most important in students' responses and prevented us from getting bogged down in idiosyncratic details.
2. They made relationships and patterns among pieces of data easier to see.
3. They made it easy to share our data with other people.

Group members received copies of everyone else's summary sheets (see Figure 2.3 for a reproduction of part of Lynne's page), and we discussed patterns we saw in them at a research-group meeting. We noticed that nearly all students across grade levels expressed positive feelings about spelling, and that many saw themselves as good spellers—findings that further corroborated our self-evaluations using the Speller's Bill of Rights. Almost every student could identify someone in his or her life who was a good speller, and they uniformly realized that even those good spellers sometimes made mistakes, which we felt was a healthy understanding.

Unfortunately, some other trends were less satisfying for us. For example, the most common response to "When is it important to spell correctly?" was "On spelling tests," except among the first graders, who hadn't experienced tests yet. A number of students were unable to articulate satisfactory reasons for correct spelling. As Lois explains it,

Kids across the board weren't as clear as we might like them to be on why spelling is important. That was an area that made us all wonder, "Wow, did I ever think this through and convey to my students why correct spelling is a standard that's important, or did I just assume that because I was teaching spelling they'd naturally make the connection?"

	Do you like figuring out words?	When is it imp. to spell correctly?	Who is a good speller?	Why?	How do people learn to spell?	How did you learn?
K.G.	nod	?	Dustin	he knows how to read	they have to know how to read	cuz I know how to read
C.G.	yes	when you're writing	Jennifer	she can read	from writing, rdg, + talking	mrs B taught us - she makes us learn
D.H.	yes - it's kind of fun	when you're rdg to teacher or parent	Jennifer	she helps us read a lot	sound 'em out	I sound them out
M.H.	yes	when you're writing a bk.	my daddy	I don't know - he writes a lot	sound words out	sounding words out
J.J.	yes	when you send a letter to someone	Definitely Jennifer.	b/c she thinks really hard	they think in their minds	I don't know
D.L	not really	when you're a grown-up	Jennifer	she knows how to read + stuff	by practicing	by pract, looking @ words, sounding out

Figure 2.3 An enlargement of sections from Lynne's one-page data summary

We realized then that it was just as important to talk about when and why to spell correctly as it was to focus on how to do so.

We also noticed that very few of our students, not even the fifth graders, could answer Question 6—"Why are words spelled the way they are?"—with any degree of sophistication. Most students said they didn't know. If they did take a guess, they tended to focus on letter-sound relationships or historical arbitrariness ("people just wanted to spell them that way"). One student even mentioned divine intervention: "Because God made them that way." Although sound and custom both play a role in our spelling system, these responses cued us to the need to teach more explicitly about how word patterns, derivations, and other meaning-based logics contribute to spelling.

Analyzing Writing from a Common Prompt

Although we were keenly interested in students' attitudes and beliefs about spelling, we knew the ultimate test of their baseline spelling achievement would be how they approached spelling tasks as writers. Consequently, we decided to gather writing samples from students in grades 1 through 5 for the same kind of whole-school analysis we did with students' question-naires. In order to make it easier to focus on students' spelling rather than on their topic choice, we asked all students to write on the following open-ended prompt (Yarmouth School Department 1998):

> You have some special people in your life: family members, relatives, school friends, teachers, coaches, etc. Choose one to write about today. Help your reader to know this person very well, as you do. Show exactly why he or she is special to you.
>
> As you write and rewrite, be sure to ask yourself the following ques-tions:

T I P

Administering a Common Prompt

Here are some suggestions for administering a writing prompt to students; they may make your spelling analysis easier.

- Have students write under the same conditions they experience dur-ing regular writing time. If they're used to being able to consult wall charts or walk around as they think, let them. Otherwise, you'll get a good sense of how they deal with test taking—not how they spell in a regular writing situation.
- Make sure that students keep all of their drafts, so you can see how their editing for spelling changes over time.
- Emphasize to students the need to cross out words they spell a sec-ond time, rather than erase them. This way, you'll be able to see the tracks of their thinking.
- Debrief the experience when students have finished, and ask them to articulate specifically how they faced spelling challenges. You might also want to ask them to write on this topic for five to ten minutes before the group discussion; this way, you'll have individual data as well.

1. Is my paper clearly written?
2. Are my ideas well organized?
3. Have I included enough specific details so that the reader gets to know my special person and understand why he or she is so special to me?
4. Does my writing show my own voice and personal expression?
5. Have I chosen the best words to express my ideas?
6. Are my sentences clear and complete?
7. Are my spelling, capitalization, and punctuation correct?

Gail downloaded this prompt from the web site of another district that had made its evaluation program for writing available to the public, but you might choose to develop your own prompt with a colleague or to use one that has been released by the makers of a standardized test. In Maine, elementary teachers annually receive the writing prompt from the previous year's test for fourth graders, as well as samples of student work at each of the six score points. A number of these prompts could be adapted for school-wide use—check and see if your state makes similar material available.

We analyzed students' writing samples in several different ways. First, teachers from the same grade level worked in pairs to combine their sets of papers and discuss them with each other. We framed our conversations in terms of students' strengths, rather than in their weaknesses, by working from the question "What do these students know about spelling?" These pairs had the opportunity to calibrate their expectations and to think about how further growth could be supported in students at their grade level. At the end of these meetings, partners divided their students' papers into three rough categories—skilled, average, and struggling spellers—in order to provide other members of the group with a sense of how achievement typically ranged in a given grade.

Then, each of us paired up with a teacher from a different grade to examine a packet of writing samples that included a paper or two from each of the three categories at each level. We felt that reading fifteen to twenty papers was manageable—enough to help us draw some conclusions about development across the school, yet not so many that we would get bogged down in unnecessary detail. The Tip on the next page, "Questions for Cross-Grade Analysis," contains some of the questions we used to guide our cross-grade discussions.

After this second set of meetings concluded, we gathered as a whole group to discuss what we had noticed. As each pair reported to the rest of us,

T I P

Questions for Cross-Grade Analysis

- How does the percentage of correctly spelled words compare from grade to grade?
- At what grade level does correct spelling become common for words that children use most often in their writing? (See Bolton and Snowball [1993a] for a list of 100 frequently used words in children's writing.)
- How do students at various levels spell the same word or words triggered by the topic? (With our samples, it was interesting to keep track of various spellings for words such as *special, friend, family*, and *favorite,* as they were commonly used in students' work across the grade levels.)
- Where, across the set of papers, do most writers at a grade level begin to use conventions such as contractions, inflectional endings, and doubled consonants? Where do most students start to control them?
- What kinds of words do older writers invent? Does their risk taking in first-draft spelling keep pace with the risk taking evident in younger writers' work?
- What kinds of editing do you notice? Do students self-correct common words? Do they make more than one attempt at words about which they're unsure?
- When students misspell words, what evidence of spelling logics do you see? Are they relying only on sound as a spelling strategy, or do their errors indicate attention to visual information and/or meaning?

Kelly recorded their findings on the chart reproduced in Figure 2.4. Although our intention in discussing developmental trends was not to create a new kind of scope and sequence for spelling instruction, we did decide to "divvy up" a few concepts that seemed most appropriately taught at a particular grade level: for example, first graders should be introduced to the idea that every word needs a vowel (or a consonant like y that functions as one). Fourth and fifth graders should explore the common derivations for words such as *signal, signature,* and *assignment.*

We were careful not to specify too many things—just the few that we felt were most important—and throughout the discussion, we kept in mind Diane's reminder of "the wonderful differences in each child's brain" and the differing "amount of exposure each child has had to print." We knew

Grade 1	• Correct spelling of high-frequency words (2 and 3 letters) • Transposing letters (e.g., *HRE* for *her*) • Confusion between *c* and *k, s* and *c*
Grade 2	• Transposing continues • Beginning and ending sounds are generally correct • *-ing* under control • Confusion about doubling consonants
Grade 3	• Each syllable is represented in most multisyllabic words • Initial blends are generally under control • Digraphs (e.g., *-ch, -sh*) are generally under control • *e*-marker words correct (e.g., *give*) • Confusion continues about doubling consonants
Grade 4	• Misspellings are consistent • Lots of self-editing/correction • Use of apostrophes not consistent (e.g., "she live's down the road")
Grade 5	• Confusion about apostrophes continues • Confusion about double vowels • "Important" big words are spelled correctly, especially brand names or city names • Students use what they know about other words (visual knowledge) but not through prefixes and suffixes or meaning
Grades 1–5	• Homonym confusion • Misspellings are often consistent with developmental stages we've read about • Kids are working hard as spellers; their mistakes are mostly logical • Evidence of risk taking • Percent of correctness increases each year • Same vowel sounds are spelled multiple ways • Sometimes they need to see difference between spoken and written language (e.g., *COUSINT* for *cousin*) • We need to ask kids when it's not clear what strategies they are using (is the child who spells *once* as *ONEC* using visual knowledge but not controlling it, or using the known word *one*?)

Figure 2.4 Some spelling trends we noticed about student writing to the school-wide prompt

that an individual child's needs could not necessarily be predicted by his or her membership in a particular grade. Nonetheless, we felt that creating a loose framework of K–5 expectations would help us coordinate our efforts more effectively and ensure that students didn't miss out on some of the crucial information they needed to become competent spellers.

We reaped a number of benefits from our analysis and discussion of the writing samples. First of all, the process helped us see what Lois calls "the whole picture":

> I really loved having the opportunity to [analyze the cross-grade samples] and want to do more of it. Seeing the levels of progress in students (especially ones you've had) was heartening. I really think educators need to see this. We could see developmental movement. Often something they just didn't get in first grade is clearly evident in second, so if you've been teaching that concept in first, you might want to sit back and say, "Hey, maybe I'm wasting everyone's time on that one. They just aren't (for the most part) ready and my expectation is out of whack."
>
> I think it really helps for everyone to see the whole picture. When it came time to set up some guidelines as to who should be doing what at which grade level, we were basing our decisions on student work, not just blindly and arbitrarily setting benchmarks.

In addition, we realized that our students' spelling was not the crisis we had assumed it to be. Lynne spoke for many of us when she wrote the following: "I feel better and more confident about us as a school [where spelling is concerned]. When we looked at samples from our grade level and then across the grade levels, I saw good spelling and good spelling attempts." Although we were certainly able to identify areas for improvement, we found it much more comfortable to take risks with our inquiry when we were not working from a position of defensiveness.

Developing a List of Spelling Strategies

One of the themes of our early conversations about spelling was that we didn't believe learning a set of rigid rules or practicing isolated skills was going to give students all the tools they needed to be confident writers. Instead, the children would need to know how to apply what they already knew to a new situation, how to use resources efficiently, and how to enlist others for help. In short, they would have to be strategic spellers in the sense described by Routman (1994): spellers who could use their skills "purposefully and independently" across a variety of contexts (135).

We all agreed with this idea in theory, but in practice many of us were nervous about whether we had enough personal knowledge—both as writers and teachers—to guide our work with students. When we discussed Wilde's sixth principle from the Speller's Bill of Rights (1996a), one member joked, "I'm not sure I 'know about and have available a lot of ways to come up with spellings.' How am I going to help kids see them?" Since more than one of us was feeling this way, we decided to devote part of a meeting to generating a list of strategies that we used (or that we'd seen kids use) for spelling an unknown word. Here's what we brainstormed:

- Ask a friend who's a good speller.
- Ask a friend or a teacher for a part of the word—the beginning, so you can find it in the dictionary, or the part of the word that's wrong.
- Ask for confirmation from a friend or teacher: Is this right?
- Ask a friend or a teacher where to find the word.
- Look in a book.
- Go to a place where the word appears (on a chart, on a sign, etc.).
- Stretch the word out; say the sounds slowly.
- Hear the word or see it in your mind.
- Think about whether it's a long or a short word.
- Use a word you already know and change it a little (e.g., *Jake, make, cake*).
- Figure out how many "chunks" or syllables the word has.
- Count the number of syllables and compare it to the syllables the spellchecker generates.
- Make sure each syllable has a vowel.
- Write a word several different ways and decide which one looks right.
- Substitute letters you know make the same sound (e.g., *ph/f, ck/c, c/s, ough/f*).
- Use a mnemonic device (e.g., the principal is your pal, a friend to the end, there's a rat in *separate*).
- Circle or underline words or parts of words you need to check.
- Write the word in the air.
- Think about the configuration (shape) of the word. Are there tall or short letters? Are there letters below the line?
- Spell the root word (e.g., *complete* for *completion*, *invite* for *invitation*).

Posted on our message board for several weeks after our meeting, this list opened up possibilities for each of us as writers as well as teachers. Although a number of the entries—for example, "look it up in the dictionary" and "ask someone who's a good speller"—were generally familiar ones, everyone found at least two or three strategies that she had not used before. We realized the same would be true of our students: a similar classwide brainstorming session would be likely to reveal new options to each child, expanding his or her options when it came time to write. Kids would therefore be able to serve as resources for each other.

We also realized that, if we were really to serve as what Vygotsky (1978) calls "the more capable other," it would be our responsibility to introduce children to useful strategies that no student in a particular class might have mentioned during the brainstorming; there would be times when we would have to add brand-new ideas to the classroom pot. We couldn't stretch students with new alternatives if our own repertoire of strategies was limited, however. These realizations reinforced the importance of pooling our knowledge as a group and then feeding that knowledge back into our practice.

T I P

Brainstorming Spelling Strategies with Your Students

1. Start with the students' own language when recording their contributions, but restate those contributions with "technical" terms so they begin to develop a language for talking about writing and editing. For example, if a student says he "goes back and fixes" a word in a second draft, talk about "self-correction." If another mentions "breaking it up into parts," use the word *syllable* so she'll be able to learn new terminology for concepts she already understands.

2. When charting your students' contributions, use children's initials to note who said what. This way, you'll be able to go back and examine the document later. You'll also be able to give public credit to children for their good ideas.

3. Make sure that everyone feels like his or her contributions are valued. If a student offers something that seems a little off the wall, try to keep him talking until you get something you can reshape that makes sense.

4. Don't be afraid to add an item to the list if you have seen a student in your class use a strategy that hasn't been mentioned. Drawing on your observations ensures that you're adding something your students really do—not just something you *think* they should do.

We returned to these ideas in subsequent meetings, sometimes opening a session by sharing anecdotes from our classrooms about student strategy use we had observed. In addition, we began to incorporate some of these strategies in our own writing. A notable example comes from our retreat, when two or three group members used the "have a go" strategy (writing a word several ways to see which looks right) repeatedly in their daily freewrites. The previous year's set of freewrites—completed before we began to work on spelling—included no evidence of this strategy. If we could adopt a strategy after simply hearing about it in a research-group meeting, how much more likely would kids be to adopt it if they were taught it in a well-crafted mini-lesson?

Pursuing a Common Reading Agenda

As teacher-researchers, we've learned to read with a slightly different mind-set than we did before. On one hand, we're always looking for ways to push our practice forward. On the other, we've learned to trust ourselves so that we're not tempted to implement slavishly all of the nifty ideas we see in print. Instead, we use our research-group discussions and our analysis of classroom-based data as ways to test what we're reading against the realities of teaching in our own context.

For two years now, we have chosen to read a number of books and articles in common, both because this practice gives us some shared knowledge and because it builds a sense of community in the group. During our first year together, we focused on readings about teacher research (Hubbard and Power 1993; Power 1996; Portalupi 1993) as we were learning to do classroom-based inquiry. When we began to work on spelling, we read and discussed most of the articles in the *Primary Voices* special issue on that topic (Wilde 1996b), as well as a few selected items from *The Reading Teacher*.

A little later in the year, everyone read Laminack and Wood's *Spelling in Use* (1996), a brief but rich book that places spelling squarely in the context of writing. Because the reading was packed with important issues, we decided on a slightly different structure for our discussions, which had been fairly unstructured up to that point. Everyone prepared for that meeting by marking two quotations with a Post-it or a tape flag that she particularly wanted to raise for the group's consideration. We began with a volunteer, then others contributed their passages when they seemed to build on the previous talk. For us, this method helped ensure that everyone's voice was heard during the meeting, and it nudged us to pay closer attention to the text we were reading. We recommend it as an easy, nonthreatening way for a group of teachers to begin consideration of an inquiry topic.

Although we stress the importance of common readings for research communities, we are also careful not to make our group feel too much like a class. We don't want members to feel overwhelmed by reading assignments—many of us have numerous commitments out of school—and we do want people to have choices about what they read. We've found that the best approach is to choose a few core readings and then to gather lots of other resources that individual teachers might select on their own, whenever they find time. At the end of our first year, members documented the books they had read or skimmed independently; nearly everyone's list included four or five titles. Some members sampled up to a dozen professional books in nine months.

In addition to our common titles, a number of other books—some of them purchased with funds from a small staff-development grant—circulated among the group. For example, several members read *The Violent E and Other Tricky Sounds* (Hughes and Searle 1997) after Martha piqued their interest with a booktalk on it during a group meeting. Richard Gentry's *My Kid Can't Spell!* (1997) made the rounds from Peggy, its original owner, to Gail, Judy, Kelly, and Jill. During our summer retreat, Enola, Lynne, and Lois read and discussed the spelling sections in *Thinking and Learning Together* (1995), Bobbi Fisher's excellent book on teaching first grade. Our Appendix A includes several lists of resources we recommend on both teaching spelling and classroom-based inquiry.

This reading served a variety of functions for us. First, it helped us feel more confident about questioning conventional wisdom regarding spelling. When other teachers and researchers echoed our concerns and expressed our hopes in print, our resolve to improve our practice was strengthened. As Lynne explains, "From the reading I think we've gotten vindication that children will learn better and retain more if it's their learning, if they're not spoonfed and forced to memorize lists for a test."

Our reading was also a source of potential research questions, as the Interludes in this book demonstrate. Diane decided to investigate how her kindergartners would attempt to spell a pictured word because she had read about this approach in *Spelling in Use*. Kim made a similar choice after reading about weekly spelling meetings in the same book. Lorna's interest in the "have a go" sheets was sparked by her reading of Regie Routman's chapter on spelling in *Invitations* (1994).

Sometimes our reading led us to try one thing and then to move in another direction, as in Lois's case. Lois had read about word walls in Bolton and Snowball's work (1993a, 1993b), but she ran into trouble when she tried to implement one with her first graders:

> I had read about word walls in several professional books and thought they could be a great aid for beginning writers in my first grade. A little bank of words that were spelled correctly would probably help some of them to "get going," as it were, with their own stories. I was specifically thinking about Shawn, who always wanted to wander around behind me (with Jacques behind HIM!), asking me to spell every word that he needed to tell a story.
>
> We started by brainstorming words together that the children were using in their writing quite frequently, such as *the, love, my,* and *friend.* Then we added some lists of words that were in the same family (for example, *-all* and *-at* words) and words that included digraphs such as *sh-* and *th-*. All of these were listed by category on the bulletin board, which took up one whole wall in the room. If individual kids came to me needing a word, we'd add it to the wall. Sometimes the children would add a *th-* word or a word in the *-all* family that they had found in their reading.
>
> Well, the word wall was a success . . . if I was looking for pieces of writing with the words all spelled correctly (and no voice, and no risks, and nothing interesting to say). Children like Shawn became *tied* to the God-awful wall. If it wasn't on the wall, they weren't writing it; they weren't going to take any chances on it not being spelled right!
>
> I remember thinking, "Well, nobody put that in all these stories about the wonders of word walls!" And then mine came down. I stapled the papers together and hung them in a corner of the room where the children could still have access to them, but they became less and less a factor when their place of importance (a great big bulletin board!) was reduced and the kids had to dig to use them.
>
> I couldn't do away with it entirely—Shawn would have had a stroke! It was kind of like nicotine patches: We had to wean ourselves gradually from our dependence on the word wall.

As an alternative way to address spelling, Lois began asking kids to generate patterns of words using the morning message as a starting point. Later on, as students became more independent, she decided to shift to "sharing the pen" with them based on another reading she did: an article about interactive writing by several primary-grade educators (Button, Johnson, and Furgerson 1996). Although she ended up having to adjust her use of this technique as well, her professional reading continued to be a source of fresh inspiration and challenge for her.

The combination of our reading and close examination of our students' work also helped us resolve a conflict regarding stages of spelling development. We were familiar with the work of several scholars (Gentry 1982; Buchanan 1989) who described the features of each stage and explained how teachers might work with young writers who exhibit those characteristics. Other books we read (Bean and Bouffler 1997; Laminack and Wood 1996) de-emphasized stages because they reduced complex learning to a lockstep progression of growth that few students exhibited.

Through our research-group talk, we were able to articulate a compromise position that felt comfortable to us. There certainly did seem to be a predictable trajectory of development across our samples and observations, yet at the same time, we saw many examples of students' spelling that didn't fit the stages and many situations in which we needed other information to explain the phenomena in front of us. At some point, we began to question the usefulness of the label "transitional spelling" (Gentry 1982), when seemingly every child in our classes, from first grade to fifth, generated spellings that could be classified in this way! Consequently, we recommend that other teachers become familiar with the research on spelling stages as a way to sensitize themselves to patterns in their data, but we also suggest a healthy skepticism about such schemata, as well as careful attention to each speller as an individual learner.

Developing Research Plans

Once we engaged in the activities described in the previous pages, a number of group members had confidence enough in their knowledge base about spelling to begin to articulate individual paths for inquiry. Questions had arisen at each step we'd taken as a group, and it was time to explore them more fully with our students.

The first phase for us in developing research plans was often simply to generate more questions. Figure 2.5 is a web that Kelly and Diane created

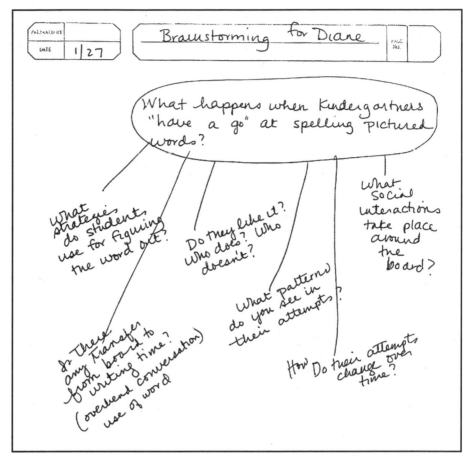

Figure 2.5 Brainstorming for Diane Smith's research question

using Diane's initial wondering, "What happens when kindergartners 'have a go' at spelling pictured words?" as their starting point. When Judy was considering inquiry about how her second graders selected words they wanted to learn, several other issues were raised by the group, including how she might find teaching points in those student-generated lists as well as what strategies might help students to make better choices.

Once someone was fairly certain about the questions she wanted to pursue, other members of the group helped her both to "tweak" them—our term for fine-tuning the language of the questions—and to develop a plan of action. For example, when Kim brought her question ("What happens when fourth graders write down words they're interested in and bring them to a weekly spelling discussion?") to the group, we helped her make the following list of ways she could collect data to answer it:

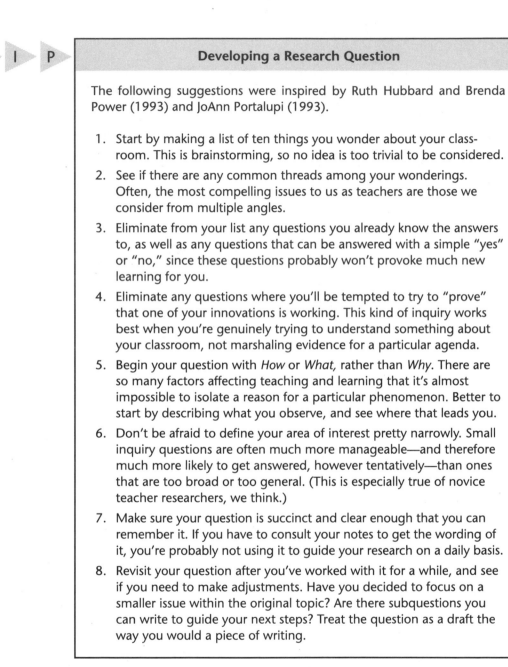

T I P

Developing a Research Question

The following suggestions were inspired by Ruth Hubbard and Brenda Power (1993) and JoAnn Portalupi (1993).

1. Start by making a list of ten things you wonder about your classroom. This is brainstorming, so no idea is too trivial to be considered.

2. See if there are any common threads among your wonderings. Often, the most compelling issues to us as teachers are those we consider from multiple angles.

3. Eliminate from your list any questions you already know the answers to, as well as any questions that can be answered with a simple "yes" or "no," since these questions probably won't provoke much new learning for you.

4. Eliminate any questions where you'll be tempted to try to "prove" that one of your innovations is working. This kind of inquiry works best when you're genuinely trying to understand something about your classroom, not marshaling evidence for a particular agenda.

5. Begin your question with *How* or *What,* rather than *Why.* There are so many factors affecting teaching and learning that it's almost impossible to isolate a reason for a particular phenomenon. Better to start by describing what you observe, and see where that leads you.

6. Don't be afraid to define your area of interest pretty narrowly. Small inquiry questions are often much more manageable—and therefore much more likely to get answered, however tentatively—than ones that are too broad or too general. (This is especially true of novice teacher researchers, we think.)

7. Make sure your question is succinct and clear enough that you can remember it. If you have to consult your notes to get the wording of it, you're probably not using it to guide your research on a daily basis.

8. Revisit your question after you've worked with it for a while, and see if you need to make adjustments. Have you decided to focus on a smaller issue within the original topic? Are there subquestions you can write to guide your next steps? Treat the question as a draft the way you would a piece of writing.

- scripting the weekly discussions
- keeping charts listing the words that were "interesting," the names of students who volunteered them, and their reasons for selection
- writing in her teaching journal about her observations

- checking students' spelling notebooks
- monitoring students' writing for appearance of the chosen words
- making video- or audiotapes of the weekly discussions
- interviewing selected students about their opinions of the discussions

Although the inquiry project that Kim eventually carried out didn't include *all* of these data sources, the plan she sketched out with help from the group served as an important starting point. Like other members who brought their emerging research plans to the group for critique and feedback, she was able to think through her individual project in more complex ways because of contributions from everyone else.

Moving Toward Shared Responsibility and a Self-Extending System

Inquiring with each other in these ways helped us see how our work with a particular group of students built on the previous work of our partners (whether they were parents or other teachers), as well as set the stage for our colleagues' future efforts. Researching as a team reminded us that we were teaching as a team, too, and therefore no one was independently responsible for students' total literacy growth.

This realization sparked seemingly contradictory reactions in us as group members: On one hand, we felt less anxious about what faced us, but on the other, we felt an accountability to each other that pushed us to work harder and be better teachers. We began to see ourselves as part of a continuum of growth, with the ultimate endpoint being students' ability to develop what Fountas and Pinnell (1996) describe as a "self-extending system of strategies" (157), or the ability to learn more about spelling from spelling.

At the same time, we were developing our own self-extending system—in this case, learning to teach spelling better through reflections on our own practice and collaboration with each other. Once that mechanism for growth was in place, there was no longer any need to rely on an externally developed spelling series or a computer program like Freddie Phoneme. Instead, we could rely on our collective expertise and the knowledge we gained from systematic, careful investigations.

This doesn't mean, however, that our initial inquiry provided us with quick and easy answers to our nagging questions about spelling. Much to the contrary: The group data we analyzed led to more questions that could only be answered by further observations of and interactions with our students—a topic we take up in the next chapter.

Extensions

1. Use the Speller's Bill of Rights to self-evaluate your spelling practice. Agree to share your results with a colleague or group of colleagues, or better yet, discuss the nine principles in kid-friendly language with your students to gain their perspectives on which rights are best "protected" in your classroom.
2. Develop your own set of survey questions for students about their attitudes toward and experiences with spelling, and then summarize the information on a single page in a manner of your choice. If you can find another teacher or two to do the same activity, compare the trends from their one-page summaries with those from your own class. We recommend this as a particularly easy way to begin data analysis.
3. Enlist another colleague to read and discuss one of our recommended resources with you. If you can't find time to meet face to face, you might lend each other a book with comments and questions marked on Post-its; the other person can respond in writing to this streamlined version of a dialogue journal. We'd also be interested in chatting with you about your spelling reading as well; e-mail Gail at gibsong@supt.sad1.k12.me.us, and she can forward your message to other members of the group.
4. Use a three-column chart like the following to help you think through a potential research plan:

Questions I Have About Spelling in My Class	Subquestions that Relate to My Main Question	Ways I Could Collect Data to Answer My Questions

INTERLUDE

Developing Word Awareness and Strategies with Weekly Spelling Meetings

KIMBERLEY WRIGHT, GRADE 4

Last fall, I was frustrated by how my spelling program, which was structured around a spelling basal at the time, focused almost entirely on surface-level correctness. I wanted to get to the root of spelling matters, such as how kids develop multiple strategies to get to the correct spellings of words and how to help them be more responsible spellers in all situations—not just the ones they were graded for. There had to be more effective ways to teach spelling, but I didn't know where to start or what to do.

When our teacher-research group read *Spelling in Use* (Laminack and Wood 1996), one idea in that book particularly appealed to me. A third-grade teacher in New York City set aside one period per week to focus on spelling. He asked the students to bring some words to discuss at what he called a "class meeting." They talked about interesting words or words they were curious about, and they charted different ways to spell the same sounds. This sounded like something my fourth graders and I could do.

When I presented my plan to drop the spelling basal and tests in exchange for weekly discussions, my students were excited about it. Wide smiles spread across various faces. "You mean we don't have to use the book anymore?" they asked, incredulous. "No more spelling homework or tests to study for?" I really think they were so excited because they thought they were going to get out of some work. Little did they—or I—know that this would not be the case. Nor did I know that my original conception of the meeting would change so much as my observations of and conversations with students suggested new directions.

When I introduced the idea of spelling meetings to the students, I explained that they would be responsible for recording three words they were interested in or wondering about—words that were hard to spell or words that made them curious. They would share these words at our weekly spelling meetings, and we would choose one of those words to focus on for our lesson. I gave an example by pulling a word from a student's chapter book, and we made some observations about it, so they would have a model. I looked forward to the perfect spelling meeting where all the kids would have recorded their words and reasons why they were chosen. I looked forward to the spelling revelations, or teachable moments, from which the lesson could be extended.

That Thursday, I checked to see that each of the kids had three words. About half the class had words recorded—not an outstanding participation level. Next, the kids took turns sharing words they chose. I recorded the words on chart paper along with the student's name and reason for choosing the word. Responses were varied. Kurt shared the word *scrumptious* because he liked the way it sounded. Ilsa chose *correction* because she liked the "sound of the ending—it sounds like it should be spelled *shone*." Jan chose the word *region* because "it ends in *i-o-n,* and that ending is challenging to say," and Cara chose *prescription* because "it has three syllables and is a long word."

As I recorded words on the chart, I waited for the spelling revelation from which to extend this lesson. Nothing came. Students started to lose their focus. As the lesson continued, I began to wonder just where it was going. To make matters worse, a parent was visiting the classroom, and I worried that she might be asking herself, "What's the point in all this?" I comforted myself with the thought that it was a lesson in word awareness, and we closed with instructions to bring another three words to the next spelling meeting. At least it was a start.

The next meeting was similar, except that even fewer children had three words recorded in their notebooks. I wondered if this was going to be one of those assignments kids don't complete for a variety of excuses: "My notebook is at home"; "I forgot"; or the one that gets my blood pressure up the quickest, "I didn't do it?" as they shrug their shoulders.

Fortunately, we persisted, and the third meeting did offer an opportunity for a teachable moment. When Abigail shared the word *mousse,* I, like many of the students, pictured the animal, *moose,* but she went on to explain that she had chosen the word because "when you say it, sometimes people might think it's the animal, but this is the kind of mousse you put in your hair." After a few other students had shared, we went back to Abigail's word and talked about it being a homonym. We got out our Quick-Word books (Forest and Sitton 1998) and turned to the section on homonyms. I read *A Chocolate Moose for Dinner,* Fred Gwynne's (1976) book that plays with idioms, and the students loved it. "Wouldn't it be neat to write our own book with idioms?" I asked, and we decided to go ahead with it. We wrapped up the lesson by brainstorming idioms of our own, and then the students created a wonderful book of their own, with each student writing and illustrating a page. For the first time in our spelling meetings, we'd found an avenue to be traveled that was suggested by the words students brought to the weekly spelling meeting.

By the time our next spelling meeting came along, most students had their three words recorded. They had a clearer understanding of expectations for the assignment and a better idea of how the meeting was going to operate. A level of trust had been established that made it easier to share and be enthusiastic. It wasn't long before we had to make another adjustment, however.

A couple of weeks later, I walked around the room and randomly flipped through notebooks just before we began our meeting. While many students had done the assignment as I expected, some students simply recorded words at the last minute as I walked by and checked them. Others didn't have their notebooks at all. One student had used the previous week's list since he was absent that day and didn't share it. Then I noticed something that really surprised me. A number of students had jotted down three words ahead, and some had enough recorded for the next two or three weeks! The three words were listed, and a line was drawn to separate those words from the next list of three. On the day we had spelling meetings, they planned to record the dates.

I talked to the kids about this. If they were writing words ahead, not recording at all, or using last week's list for this week, wasn't that defeating the whole purpose of our lessons? In one instance, it had become a game: "Look, I've got enough words for the next three weeks!" "So? I've got enough for the next *six* weeks!" I reminded the students that the purpose was to record words that were difficult to spell and to be more aware of words on a consistent basis while they were reading and writing.

This was a red flag that we needed to make a change. When I checked back in my notes to chase a nagging idea I'd had, I realized I'd strayed from my original intention for kids to raise their awareness of strategy use by recording *how* they got to the correct spellings of previously misspelled words. It was the strategy, not the word, that mattered most. This is the direction we decided to take next. We called this the "Catch Yourself Using a Spelling Strategy" assignment. For the next meeting, I asked students to record at least two words they self-corrected and how they determined the correct spellings.

When the next week came around, many of the students were prepared to share words they had self-corrected and recorded. Their responses showed that they could use a variety of effective strategies. Cara needed to know how to spell *excellent* for a thank-you letter. She sounded it out and wrote it down. It didn't look right, so she asked her friend Jan for help. Jan showed Cara what was wrong with the word and helped her correct it. Another student, Ilsa, used the word *sparkles* in a story she was writing. She wasn't sure about the ending of the word, she explained, so "I wrote it three different ways. I chose the one that looked the most correct. I showed it to my mom, and it was right." Bob needed to know how to spell the word *aluminum* for a social studies test. "I couldn't spell it on the test, so I looked back at the test paper and found it." While writing in his personal journal, Joe remembered seeing the word *existence* in a book he'd been reading. He looked back in the book, found it, and wrote it correctly.

For the next few meetings, this arrangement worked better, sparking more conversation about strategies. The class seemed to lose focus after a few students had shared, though, which I took as a sign that we needed to make another adjustment. One student suggested we chart ways to remember how to spell tricky words such as *Wednesday* (*Wed-nes-day*) and *friend* ("a friend is a friend till the *-end*"). Another idea, to record various spellings for the same sound, seemed even more promising, and we decided to pursue it. We started with /shun/, which I recorded at the top of a sheet of chart paper. "What letter combinations can represent this sound?" I asked. Promptly, students called, "*-t-i-o-n*," and "*-s-i-o-n*." We made one column for each of these letter combinations and then brainstormed words that fell into each category. Some children had their dictionaries out, and they were searching for words with the right ending. Eventually, we discovered yet another letter combination that made the same sound: *-cean*, as in *ocean*.

The next week, we chose a letter combination that presented itself in a word Carter shared, *hamburger*. We focused on the /er/ sound and charted various letter combinations that represented it. A question arose whether rhyming words needed to have the same letter combinations. We didn't get into that discussion too deeply, but what a wonderful way to be led! We also thought of another extension and reinforcement activity: Since the numerous charts were beginning to pile up, why couldn't we combine the information from the charts into a class spelling guide? We ended this lesson excited and filled with awareness of the /er/ sound and how it could be represented several ways. Unfortunately, we were coming to the close of the school year.

To assess how students felt about our changed approach to spelling, I asked them to complete a survey. The data revealed that many students appreciated and grew from our sharing and charting words. The best thing that Cara liked about the change was that "we're sharing our strategies with the class." The spelling meetings helped Myles improve his spelling because he realized that "the strategies the kids in my class use, I can use." Jay learned that "there might be words that you need right up there on the charts," so he could use them as a resource. Abigail wrote, "When the teacher writes the words on the board, I see how they are spelled, and I remember them." Also a visual learner, Barry made a similar comment: "I forget how to spell words sometimes. Then when I see the words, I remember." Joe felt that recording information about his spelling helped him improve because "I see where I made my mistakes." Finally, Ilsa spoke most eloquently on the subject:

> Teachers need to know how kids are doing in spelling, and spelling meetings are a good way to find out. Recording information about my spelling has helped me to become a better speller because I think more about the word that I spelled incorrectly, and I can share it with others. I think when we started doing the spelling meeting, I learned a lot more about spelling than with the spelling tests. Spelling meetings help me think about my spelling strategies and other people's strategies, and I learn more about spelling.

My original question was "What happens when students jot down words they are wondering about or interested in, and bring them to a weekly spelling discussion?" My current answer is "Plenty," as long as their teacher is willing to make adjustments based on the data that gets generated every week. During spelling meetings, students work as a community of learners, yet they maintain an individual focus based on their needs. They can be guided into places they discovered on their own but wouldn't necessarily have found without the support and challenge of the group's collaboration.

CHAPTER 3

Do Ostrich *and* Partridge *Really Rhyme? Inquiring About Spelling with Our Students*

As we built our knowledge about spelling through our research-group investigations and our professional reading, we began to see our students' work in the classroom through fresh lenses. We realized that the children's behavior was often more strategic than we had previously assumed: Many of them knew more than we thought they did! At the same time, we saw new roles for ourselves in assisting them to develop even more sophisticated understandings of the spelling system. There was a good deal to celebrate—and a good deal more growth that could take place—for nearly every student in our care.

In April, Jill documented the following observations in her third-grade classroom:

> At our morning meeting, Garrett was telling about seeing a partridge. He wanted to write about it later, so he needed to know how to spell it. Adam said, "Well, that's easy. It starts with *p-a-r-t*." Ray said maybe it was just *p-a-r-* but everyone agreed it was *p-a-r-t*.
>
> Doug commented on the sound of *-idge*: "Is it *-i-g* or *-i-j*?" Tracey said, "It's *r-i-d-g-e*. I know because my shirt says 'Dinosaur Ridge.'" "Wow! That's a big help," said Garrett. He wrote it on the board to see if it looked right while Wade checked in the dictionary to make sure.
>
> Later on, during our writing workshop, Craig needed to know how to spell *ostrich* for his animal report. "Oh, that's easy," said Maren.

"Yeah," said Doug. "It rhymes with *partridge* and we just figured out how to spell that big word."

"Wait a minute, guys," I interrupted. "Let me say the word again. *Os-trich*" (I emphasized the /ch/ sound). "Oh, that's easy," said Craig. "It's *a-w*.""No, wait," said Billy. "I think it's *o-s*."

Elena, one of the better spellers in the room, had been sitting back quietly, listening. She silently moved to the back of the room where our wildlife kit was stored. Meanwhile Paul was helping Craig finish the word: "We know it's *o-s*. Now I think it's *t-r* because of the trrr sound," he said. Craig wrote *o-s-t-r*. "Now what?" he asked.

Elena made her way up to Craig's desk with the ostrich wildlife card, which she nonchalantly handed to him. "Here you go," she said. "It probably has some information you can use, too." Then she went back to her seat to continue her work while Craig wrote *o-s-t-r-i-c-h*. "There, that looks right. Thanks, guys."

For us, Jill's narrative represents some key ideas about what happens when teachers inquire with their students about spelling:

- Spelling becomes a rich topic of conversation for the entire class to explore.
- Students become resources for each other, rather than the teacher being the only source of assistance.
- Teachers are able to observe what their students know about spelling in meaningful, communication-centered contexts.
- Opportunities arise for teachers to stretch students with carefully-timed interventions.

Because this example is such an evocative one, we've decided to use it as a touchstone for the rest of this chapter. We'll discuss each of the four ideas in turn, introducing them as they played out with Jill's students and then connecting them to classroom examples experienced by other members of the research group. We hope you'll get a sense of the kinds of things we learned from our inquiry, as well as a glimpse at the roles played by each teacher when she decided to let the children's questions and insights drive her spelling curriculum. When the children joined us as co-researchers, both our research and their educations were enriched.

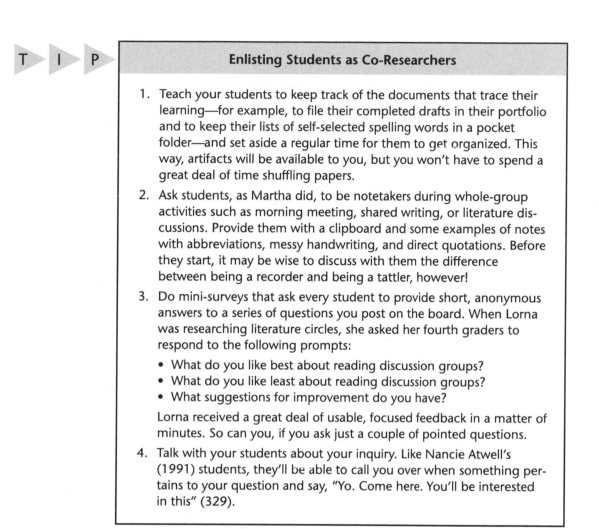

T   I   P

Enlisting Students as Co-Researchers

1. Teach your students to keep track of the documents that trace their learning—for example, to file their completed drafts in their portfolio and to keep their lists of self-selected spelling words in a pocket folder—and set aside a regular time for them to get organized. This way, artifacts will be available to you, but you won't have to spend a great deal of time shuffling papers.

2. Ask students, as Martha did, to be notetakers during whole-group activities such as morning meeting, shared writing, or literature discussions. Provide them with a clipboard and some examples of notes with abbreviations, messy handwriting, and direct quotations. Before they start, it may be wise to discuss with them the difference between being a recorder and being a tattler, however!

3. Do mini-surveys that ask every student to provide short, anonymous answers to a series of questions you post on the board. When Lorna was researching literature circles, she asked her fourth graders to respond to the following prompts:
   - What do you like best about reading discussion groups?
   - What do you like least about reading discussion groups?
   - What suggestions for improvement do you have?

   Lorna received a great deal of usable, focused feedback in a matter of minutes. So can you, if you ask just a couple of pointed questions.

4. Talk with your students about your inquiry. Like Nancie Atwell's (1991) students, they'll be able to call you over when something pertains to your question and say, "Yo. Come here. You'll be interested in this" (329).

Spelling Becomes a Rich Topic for Whole-Class Conversation

Garrett asked how to spell *partridge* as a part of morning meeting, a daily time when Jill's third graders gathered on the rug for a few minutes to share news and artifacts from their lives. Because he planned to write about his experiences later during workshop time, the conversation shifted from his family hunting trip to ways he could spell the word he needed. Everyone in the room heard Tracey describe her strategy for using environmental print, and everyone was welcome, because of the open-ended format of the meeting, to offer other suggestions to Garrett. Not only was the discussion a way for information about strategies to be shared, it was also a community-building experience in Jill's class. When the conversation continued during writing time, students were able to use talk as a way to explore and test their options as spellers.

Other members of the research group decided to plan deliberately for whole-class conversations about spelling. Although our initiatives were different depending upon our students' grade level and experience base as writers, at the core of each initiative was our common belief that students could learn a lot about spelling from each other. We realized that one of the biggest weaknesses of the spelling series some of us had used previously was that so little time was allowed for exploratory talk. Later, after we adopted a student-centered philosophy, most of our spelling instruction took place on an individual basis, during writing conferences, so there wasn't much opportunity for students to share ideas then, either.

After our research-group brainstorm about spelling strategies (see Chapter 2), Enola asked her second graders to make a similar list of ways they used to figure out how to spell an unknown word. She recorded students' contributions in their own language and labeled them with their initials. This technique allowed her to use the chart as an assessment tool, as well as to give students "credit" for their good ideas. After the discussion was finished, she hung the sheet on the wall, where it served as a resource for writers throughout the year. Not only did this activity produce a useful document, but it also generated a great deal of conversation as students explained their different approaches. This talk, as much as the published list, helped the children expand their repertoire of spelling strategies.

After she observed that her fifth graders rarely used meaning-based spelling strategies, Gail planned a discovery lesson around prefixes. The whole group generated a list of common prefixes such as *pre-, re-, un-,* and *il-,* and then heterogeneous teams of four students investigated one prefix in preparation for teaching a mini-lesson to the rest of the class. For Gail, that small-group talk was just as illuminating as the whole-class brainstorming. "It was a good assessment time for me," she says, "because I learned that some of them didn't understand exactly what a prefix was. They thought if the combination of letters appeared in a word, it was automatically a prefix. So if they saw a word like *preach,* they put it in their *pre-* list." Fortunately, students who did understand the difference were able to explain it to their classmates during their group discussions. According to Gail, students also "pilfered some of the root words from each other during small-group work. Because the room was small, they could hear each other's conversations. So if one group was talking about the word *rearrange*, another group might add *prearrange* to their lists."

Since the point of the small groups was to prepare for teaching the rest of the class, not simply to generate long lists of words, students hit upon the strategy of using their words in sentences to help each other determine the meaning of the prefixes. "What was funny and, I guess, serendipitous," Gail remembers, "was that several of them began with the sentences in the bottom of the dictionary entry, and truthfully, some of the others had never noticed that information before. They had only paid attention to the definitions." Both these planning conversations and the question-and-answer sessions that followed each mini-lesson helped students come to a deeper understanding of prefixes—and, quite by accident, the dictionary—than they would have gained through listening to a teacher-led lesson.

Sometimes, opportunities for class discussion presented themselves in unusual ways, as Kim found out with her fourth graders one day during physical education class:

> As we were doing the pelican stretch (left hand on the wall, right leg up, knees together, pushing gently down from the quadricep), I asked the kids which muscle we were stretching. "Quadricep," they answered rather quietly. (It was a sleepy gray morning.)
>
> "What is it?" I asked them again, slightly raising the volume of my voice.
>
> "Quadricep!" they hollered back.
>
> "Spell it!" I replied, and the students hesitated only a second before several attempts were made. I listened as they called out various guesses. Finally, they asked me what the right answer was, but I didn't tell them. Instead, I charged them to jot a spelling of the word down on a piece of paper and bring it to class the next day.
>
> When we returned to class, many of the students eagerly attempted correct spellings of *quadricep*. They wrote it different ways to see which one looked right; they used dictionaries; and they also asked to borrow the book from which I take many of my lessons for physical education. They knew they could find it there!
>
> During our reading/writing time the next afternoon, we charted the various spellings of the word. Students took turns writing down what they came up with. What was really interesting was how individual stu-

T ▷ I ▷ P ▷

Making Time for Notetaking

Being a teacher-researcher of spelling (or any subject, for that matter) means collecting data. Although written data such as anecdotal records or entries in a teaching journal often provides the richest record of student learning, we know from experience how difficult it can be to find time to write in a busy classroom. Here are some strategies and shortcuts that have worked for us:

1. Use an idea from Lorna and enlist a student to make a copy for you of any document you and the students brainstorm on chart paper or the chalkboard.

2. Make some abbreviated notes in pencil on a document you're discussing with children. Lois uses this technique to record students' comments about patterns they notice in the morning message.

3. Write just a word or two on a Post-it in the middle of a conference or class discussion; we bet you'll be surprised how much detail comes back with a small piece of information to trigger it.

4. Set aside the first five to ten minutes of workshop to write along with students, and use the time to document your observations from earlier in the day. (This will also encourage independence in student writers, forcing them to consider topic choice on their own for a few minutes before they can ask for assistance from you.)

5. Enlist your instructional aide (as Gail does with her partner Vicky) to be an observer and a notetaker during important class sessions in which you'll be busy facilitating discussion. If you have regular parent volunteers, they might serve the same role.

dents recorded the way they heard the word. I think that in some cases the letters they wrote down were indeed the actual sounds those students were hearing. What a window of opportunity to talk about the "audio" aspect of spelling words! I asked one student to wait till the end to share his attempt because I knew he had spelled the word correctly (he had used my physical education book as a reference).

This activity pointed me in a direction that was interesting and helpful to pursue. The students and I began to chart various representations of sounds in all their different written forms and to keep the charts up in the room as resources. This activity was the seed from which weekly spelling meetings grew.

We urge you to follow our lead and build some whole-class talk time into your planning for spelling instruction. For us, these brainstorming and charting sessions provided a rich source of data about what students knew and could verbalize; they provided us with a new way to assess students' spelling knowledge (see Chapter 5 for more discussion of assessment and evaluation issues). They were also a way for a rich "gene pool" of ideas about spelling to be made available to every member of our classes—often in more kid-comprehensible language than we, as adult spellers, could muster.

Students Help Each Other with Spelling

Another striking aspect of Jill's story is the way her students collaborated to help their classmates spell words they needed in their writing. No one said, "Be quiet, Craig. I'm working on *my* piece," or made fun of Garrett because he couldn't spell a word that is fairly common in our rural community. Instead, both boys found themselves the beneficiary of the group's shared wisdom.

Lois saw the same kind of collaborative spirit among her first graders. Her notes during writing time included snippets of overheard conversation like the following:

"Patrick gave me 'Great White Shark.' He had it in a magazine."
"Do you know how I knew this one? Rebecca said it started like her name, and then I knew it was an *R*."
"Josh had used *tractor* in his story before, so he told me how to spell it."

Lois attributes some of the children's willingness to share their expertise with each other to their interest in her research on spelling. They gained confidence in their ability to help each other because she took their ideas seriously enough to document them. "For all of us in the classroom, I think our awareness of spelling strategies was heightened. There was a real feeling of 'Hey, if you've got a good idea, if you have a tip or a trick, if you see a pattern or technique, let's talk about it. Let's write it somewhere—it might help someone else.'"

Lynne encourages this kind of collaboration in individual writing conferences with her first graders:

If children ask for help spelling a word, I rarely spell it for them. Instead, I might tell them to write the sounds carefully: "Say the word slowly and write what you hear." I might direct them to a place in the room or school where they can find the word (e.g., the morning message, a charted poem, the bathroom for the word *boys*). If I know there's someone who's recently used the word in a piece of writing, I'd say, "Go ask Chad to help you find it in his *Bully* book." This way, even struggling writers can be a resource for others, thus giving them a sense of pride and accomplishment.

The primary kids weren't the only ones offering each other assistance. Lorna's fourth graders engaged in a great deal of peer interaction over spelling as well. If a friend asked them to, they would put dots under the letters of attempts that were correct—a technique their teacher used that enabled the speller to focus on the part of the word that needed work. Rather than simply spelling the word, they often provided each other with subtle clues: a strategy for keeping homonyms straight, another example from the same word family, the first three letters to make it easier to look the word up in the dictionary. As Lorna encouraged them to be more independent spellers, they in turn encouraged and supported more strategic behavior in each other.

We eventually discovered that students' ability to help each other was a crucial factor in *our* ability to collect data as researchers and provide writing/spelling instruction to individuals. If children needed our attention every second of the day, there was no way to observe them at work or to confer with individuals or small groups. Here's how Martha devised an innovative way to foster a climate of independence and collaborative problem solving among her third graders:

I had read about teachers who wore a special necklace to signal to students that they were unavailable. So, I prepared a baseball cap to wear by covering the advertisement with contact paper and labeling it "Taking Note." The next day I explained to my students that when I wore the cap, they were not to talk to me unless it was an emergency such as bleeding or choking. "The Cap," as it came to be known, served its purpose for most students. Still, there were those who never got the message. One or two, in particular, would come to where I was notetaking and stand, waiting to be recognized. I'd fight the urge to make eye contact with them.

The next year, having learned from my first experience with "the Cap," I took more time in training my new class of students. I explained more carefully why I sometimes needed to work without distractions. I told them that important teaching and learning happens when I'm working with a small group, and interruptions ruin everyone's concentration. I also discussed how much I learn about them during my fifteen-minute notetaking sessions.

Together, the group listed some problems that might arise and brainstormed ways they could address them without my help. When we finished, I gave students an assignment along with a choice of activities to do when they finished it. It was time for the class to practice solving problems without me. After donning "the Cap" as a signal not to disturb me, I gathered three or four students at the work table and gave them a simple task. As the small group worked, I took notes on what I could hear happening in the room with those who were working independently. After twenty minutes, we assembled as a class to debrief what problems arose and how they were handled. This new information was added to our chart.

The whole process took an hour of valuable class time, but that one-hour lesson on self-reliance lasted all year. In fact, students were so respectful of small-group and observational time that I stopped wearing my cap. Every once in a while, someone would notice that I needed uninterrupted time, and he or she would get it for me to put on.

From this experience, Martha's students learned that she wasn't the only one who could assist them, whether they needed a pencil or a listener for their newly finished draft.

For us, these examples provide a stark contrast with the days when our spelling instruction centered around solitary preparation for weekly tests. Our past practices offered little time or impetus for students to help each other with spelling; in fact, they often fostered competition rather than collaboration when certain classes of students became overly concerned with how their test performance compared to that of their peers. Kids' talk about spelling centered on "What did you get?" when the test papers were passed back, rather than on how they might help each other pursue writing for their own purposes. Moreover, our one-size-fits-all spelling curriculum made it extremely unlikely that spellers with weak natural ability would ever be able to assist their peers in the ways that we witnessed many of our students doing over the course of the past year.

Observation of Spellers Takes Place in Meaningful Contexts

Writers' workshop afforded Jill the opportunity to observe students' spelling as they engaged in the real work of writing. They weren't practicing spelling for its own sake, doing "dry-run" worksheets to prepare for far-in-the-future compositions. Instead, they were figuring out how to spell words they needed immediately, while wrestling at the same time with all of the other decisions that young writers must make around topic, audience, and focus. As Jill listened in on their conversation, she was able to contemplate how they might use their spelling skills and strategies in writing contexts outside of school—when they would no longer be able to get help from their teacher.

Other members of the research group were able to gather important data about their students' spelling when they attended to it in meaningful contexts. In several cases, we found that we had underestimated the level of correctness certain children could achieve because we had primarily assessed them in one of two situations: Either they were spelling out of the context of writing, where they were limited to only a few cues, or they were writing for an audience where correctness didn't matter. When they were invested in their work, they were often able to spell far more words conventionally.

Last year, a real-world writing task presented itself when a Mapleton resident named Mr. Kilcollins came to talk to the fifth graders about his experiences as a World War II veteran. Drafted and then edited before they were sent, students' thank-you notes provided a good look at students' spelling strategies in a meaningful context. Christina Deflore's letter (see Figure 3.1) was a particularly intriguing example. In this one-page piece of writing, Christina misspelled seven words, but she was able to correct each one of them without any assistance from her teacher, and she employed a wide range of strategies to do so. Figure 3.2 contains a key to her self-corrections developed from an interview Kelly did with Christina about the piece.

Christina is a good example of the kind of student we came to value more highly through our research process. Her particular strengths did not serve her well in a standardized testing situation in which spelling was marked as either right or wrong. On the California Test of Basic Skills (CTBS), a test that required her to select the correct spelling of a word from four choices, her score was just slightly below the national average. What the CTBS didn't reveal, however, was how close Christina's misspellings

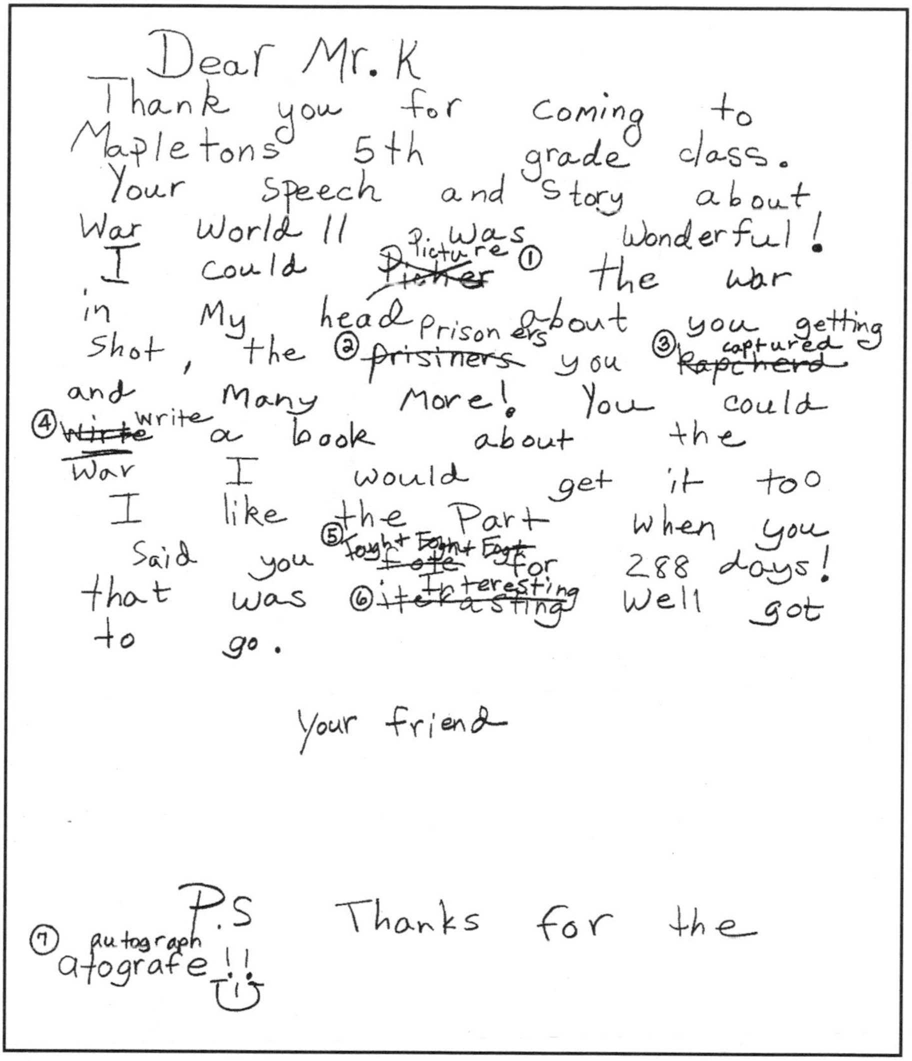

Dear Mr. K
Thank you for coming to
Mapletons 5th grade class.
Your speech and story about
War World II ?.was wonderful!
I could picture ① the war
in My head Prison ers about you getting
shot, the ② prisiners you ③ captured
and Many More! You could
④ write a book about the
War I would get it too
I like the Part when you
Said you ⑤ fought Fought for 288 days!
that was ⑥ interesting Well got
to go.

Your friend

P.S Thanks for the
⑦ autograph
afografe !!

Figure 3.1 Christina's thank-you letter

usually were (often only a letter or two off), and it didn't take into account her extraordinary ability to use spelling strategies, resources like the dictionary, or her classmates' assistance to self-correct her spelling errors. Her profile on the CTBS printout didn't reveal any of these strengths, but our research data did.

At the same time our inquiry helped us value Christina's success more highly, it also pushed us to raise our standards. We realized that students like Christina were probably capable of better spelling in a variety of situations.

1. *picture*
   CHRISTINA: *Picture* was a spelling word a while back, so I sort of forgot it until I looked at it again.

2. *prisoners*
   KELLY: How did you know to change the *i* to an *o*?
   CHRISTINA: Because *o* and *i* can make, like, the same kinds of sounds.

3. *captured*
   CHRISTINA: You know how *c* and *k* are tricky. They can sound the same. The one with the *c* looked more like it was spelled right.

4. *write*
   CHRISTINA: The *r* sounded before the *i*.

5. *fought*
   Christina used two known words that sounded the same (*got* and *thought*) in her attempts, as well as the "have a go" strategy (writing the word four times until it looked right).

6. *interesting*
   CHRISTINA: I sounded it out again, then looked it up in the dictionary. I found out I didn't have the *es* right.

7. *autograph*
   Christina used placeholder spelling with this word: "I knew it wasn't right. I just wrote it that way until I could figure it out." Then she split the compound word into its components: "I knew how to spell both parts."

Figure 3.2 Key to Christina's self-corrections

When she had an authentic purpose for writing—a thank-you letter to an adult in the community—she cared about correctness. When spelling "counted," so to speak, she was able to spell conventionally. As teachers, we needed to help our students understand that more of their writing should "count."

Gail and Kelly shared Christina's sample during a research-group meeting, and all of us marveled at the variety of strategies she controlled during the editing process. Her work was a perfect example of what we wanted students to be able to do when they left Mapleton Elementary, and we talked a great deal about what kinds of instruction had promoted her strategic behavior. Not only did we learn a lot about Christina by discussing her case with each other, but we also learned a new method for conferring with students about spelling. We could ask other students, even very young ones, to circle words they had self-corrected and discuss the strategies they used. This technique would give us valuable information about students' spelling in the context of their writing.

Teachers weren't the only ones during our inquiry, however, who had the opportunity to observe spelling for meaningful purposes. Gail's fifth

T ▶ I ▶ P ▶

Helping Students Edit for Spelling

- The right tools make editing more fun. Make sure you have plenty of correction fluid, correction tape, and supplies for cutting and pasting available to students.

- Develop a simple checklist to paste inside kids' journals or writing folders with a few questions they're responsible for answering for themselves before their writing reaches an audience. The list might include the following questions, even for inexperienced writers: Do all of your sentences end with a punctuation mark? Do your sentences begin with capital letters? Have you spelled everything the best you can, using all the resources available to you?

- Teach students to proofread their work line by line, using a piece of paper to track where they are and keep their eyes focused on a small section of the text at a time.

- Teach older children to change the size of the font they're using to word process a piece before they print it. Sometimes, seeing the words in a different place on the page can make students more aware of their errors.

- Consider photocopying drafts occasionally. As Gail found out, students whose handwriting is laborious often balk at editing their work because they don't want to have to recopy it. Editing for spelling on a copy and then carefully fixing those words on their first drafts can sometimes increase these students' motivation to edit.

- Create a known-word list (Hughes and Searle 1997) and hold students accountable for these words.

- Help kids identify words they consistently misspell, and then hold students accountable for correcting them. These words can be printed on a Post-it to keep on students' desks—a technique that makes them readily accessible while suggesting that the words aren't necessarily permanent problems.

- Help kids identify some students in the group who are "editing experts" whom they can call on for final-draft assistance.

graders were able to do the same thing when their reading partners—first graders from Lois's and Lynne's classrooms—wrote them letters after they met. In this case, the meaningful context was reciprocal. The first graders had an authentic purpose for writing to their partners, a task they took very seriously and one that allowed Lois to observe them using their best spelling strategies. The fifth graders also had an authentic purpose: to decipher their partners' invented spelling in order to understand their messages. The older children's conversations as they worked to read these letters helped Gail understand their criteria for good spelling as well as observe the language they used to talk about it in a relaxed, informal setting. Several students used their observations of the first graders' spelling to reflect on how much their own spelling had improved—more valuable information for Gail.

Since one of Peggy's practices in the resource room is to ask students to use literacy to participate in class decision making, she is often able to observe their use of spelling in a meaningful context. Last spring, for example, she asked the children to recommend some movies to show during a room party they were helping to plan. The children wrote their nominations in marker on a message board prominently displayed in the classroom. Anton, a child who usually struggled to express himself on paper, offered the following suggestion: *A LITEL PRINTS ASS*. In addition to proving a laugh for those of us in the research group who saw it, this invented spelling of *The Little Princess* revealed some important information about Anton:

1. He knew that each syllable of a word needed a vowel, even though he didn't always choose the correct one.
2. He was able to represent the blend *pr-* correctly.
3. He was more willing to take a public risk with spelling when his writing could influence his social context.

While Peggy might have learned the first two pieces of data from a worksheet or spelling test, she would have had no access to the third without observing Anton use literacy for his own purposes.

Observation of student spellers in meaningful contexts gives us a window on their futures. If the ultimate goal for our instruction is to prepare children for the situations requiring conventional spelling that they will encounter after they leave us, then it's not enough to assess their spelling when we set the conditions for the task. We also need to know how they fare when they are able to choose their own topics and audiences, when the contexts for text production more closely approximate the writing they will do outside of school. Inquiry that includes their perspectives on these choices will help us determine the best ways to support them as spellers.

Opportunities Arise for Carefully Timed Interventions

Some of Jill's third graders struggled to spell *ostrich* in part because they weren't saying it correctly. If Jill hadn't been monitoring their conversation, she would not have been able to step in at just the right time and say, "Let *me* pronounce the word." Her careful articulation of the ending sound helped them see the difference between *partridge* and *ostrich* (although, admittedly, careful articulation didn't do much to aid Craig with those tricky vowel sounds!). Her intervention was minor, but it came at a crucial time, and it helped her students problem solve through their spelling.

Other members of the research group found that their inquiry stance enabled them to intervene at crucial times in students' learning. Instead of relying solely on a preestablished plan for instruction that sometimes over- or underestimated students' development, we found ourselves better able to target lessons to the right children at the right time when our decisions were based on data we gathered on the spot.

Sometimes, group members started with a plan and shifted it as their analysis of the situation suggested another direction. After hearing about "have a go" sheets from Judy, as well as from Lorna, Martha decided to teach her third graders how to use them. Students had recently written on a common prompt in science, so she pulled a list of words that class members had most frequently misspelled and asked students to tackle them in pairs. She instructed students to make two or three attempts at each word, discussing them as they went along, then to check them in the dictionary.

As it turned out, the most important lesson of the day was not how to generate several options for an unknown word but how to confirm their best guesses using the dictionary. "I assumed they had dictionary skills," Martha remembers, "because at various times during the day when we were talking about words, a student would say, 'I'll check that,' and come back with the word." As she observed students checking their final attempts on their "have a go" sheets, Martha realized that many students "did not know how to use guide words to narrow in on their choices; they simply paged through from the front of the book till they hit the right section." These observations led to another lesson, in which Martha showed students how to use the boldface guide words that indicated the first and last words on each page. By asking questions such as "If the word begins with M, are you going to start at the front of the book? the back?" she also nudged them to think more strategically about their dictionary approach.

One of Lorna's interventions took the form of a series of mini-lessons based on data she gathered from her fourth graders. As Lorna remembers, these lessons "evolved from a class meeting about strategies they could use to help them become better spellers. 'Spelling rules' was added to the list, but, interestingly enough, no one at that point could give an example. I volunteered the '*i* before *e*' rule because it was one that had always stuck with me. They were not familiar with it." As she conferred with students and examined their "have a go" sheets, Lorna learned that many children were also unfamiliar with the other three rules that Wilde (1992) cites as fairly consistent (and therefore worth direct instruction): (1) dropping *e* before suffixes; (2) changing *y* to *i* before suffixes; and (3) doubling consonants before suffixes.

Consequently, Lorna taught each of these rules in brief, focused mini-lessons. At the end of the school year, she and the class had a debriefing session at which students made the following comments about the impact of this instruction on their spelling:

"When you told us the rules . . ., I started using them."
"It showed us what kind of words we needed to work on."
"I used them to check my spelling on a rough draft."

In addition to observing groups, we discovered that close attention to individual spellers at work could lead to fruitful insight and interventions. For example, when Kelly visited Kim's classroom during writers' workshop, fourth grader Devon Hall asked Kelly to help him edit a piece on NFL quarterback Steve Young. He needed to know the correct spelling for the word *position*, which he had written as *posison*. Rather than asking him to check the dictionary, Kelly asked him to think of other words he already knew how to spell that ended with the same sound. Devon brainstormed *action*, which he wrote correctly, and *motion*, which he didn't. After Kelly told him he was right about *action* and advised him to use that knowledge for the other words, he was able to self-correct both *motion* and *position*. "That looks right," he said, as he added the last letters to the second word. Then he went off to check the dictionary to confirm his attempt. A few seconds later, Kelly heard him say, "Hee hee hee, it *is* right" under his breath.

Several months later, when Devon had moved on to fifth grade, Gail overheard him telling a friend how to spell the word *billion*: "If you can spell *million*, it's the same thing." Not only had he learned a valuable strategy during Kelly's intervention that he was able to use again himself, but he was also able to explain his new knowledge to another person, and therefore to serve as a resource for his peer.

We've come to believe that some of the most lasting lessons about spelling are those that could never be scripted ahead of time in a teacher's planbook. Through observation and conferences, we've learned to be more responsive to students' needs as they unfold in front of us. When unexpected opportunities to present new information to students arise, we're more likely to intervene and capitalize on them than we were before our inquiry heightened our awareness of spelling. Diane speaks for all of us in this respect: "After years of trying every which way to teach the letters of the alphabet, I came to the conclusion that a teacher can lecture and present all she wants, but children only hear what they have need for and what matters to them. The only way to know what matters to them is to be a part of their world, which may mean forsaking some of our marvelous plans."

At the same time, we know it's our responsibility to create situations in which students' learning can leap forward. It's not enough to wait in the wings of our classroom until a "teachable moment" raises its head. While kids need to construct their own understandings, there's a good deal we can do with our modeling, our questioning, and our choice of materials or assignments that will lead them to certain kinds of discoveries more easily.

Ready to Be Researchers

Taking an inquiry stance with our students made fundamental changes in our teaching of spelling. We replaced some of the talking we had done in the past with more watching and listening. We solicited students' input about future directions and asked them to give us feedback on our experimentations with spelling instruction. They often validated what we'd tried, giving us more conviction to continue, but it was just as helpful when they didn't, as Lorna explains:

When I felt things weren't going the way I thought they should (whatever way that was), I went to the kids for help in answering my questions. They were positive and honest, even when they didn't like something. They helped me realize that whatever I tried was not going to be a complete failure—not only was I going to learn something, but the kids were, too.

As Lorna points out, our inquiry was enriched by students' participation, but so was their education. Because they were our co-researchers, we were able to plan instruction that was more responsive to their needs, more appropriate for where they were as learners than any curriculum designed by someone for a generic group of children. At the same time, we were able to demonstrate for them on a daily basis what it means to be a questioner, someone who ponders her place in the world and who considers the significance of patterns and themes. Since these are attitudes we hope students will adopt for themselves, it is crucial that we enact them in our daily work with our classes and with each other. By opening up our research process to them, we were able to serve as models of engaged, collaborative learners.

For these reasons, we encourage you to involve your students in your inquiry about spelling. You may choose to ask them for their perspectives on questions you're pursuing, as Lorna did, or you may want to ask the children to generate the questions about spelling in the first place. Either way, we predict that you'll find the same energy waiting to be tapped that Gail discusses in this excerpt from a journal entry:

> I couldn't wait to get back to my classroom to share with my kids what we were talking about in our meetings, because I knew they would be interested. I knew it would pique their curiosity. They were all ready to be researchers and couldn't wait to be part of that inquiry process.

What could be more powerful than that?

Extensions

1. Look back at the story from Jill's classroom that begins this chapter. Make a list of all the spelling strategies her students used and compare it to the list you generated with your students or your colleagues as part of the Extensions for Chapter 2. If your students don't consistently use all of the strategies you listed, you may want to plan mini-lessons around the ones they overlook.
2. Examine your weekly instructional plan and see if you can build in regular time to observe student spellers at work and/or schedule an oppor-

tunity for whole-class talk about spelling. Share your notes or your charts (initialing students' contributions makes it easier to analyze them later) with a colleague.

3. Interview a student about the logic behind his or her self-corrections, as Kelly did with Christina. Keep a list of the strategies he or she discusses and point those out at the end of the interview, perhaps suggesting one or two options that weren't mentioned. You might also consider asking students, particularly those with a fair amount of control over conventional spelling, to create a key for their self-corrections that resembles the one in Figure 3.2. A document like this one could easily be included in students' portfolios as evidence of their growth.

INTERLUDE

Creating a Climate of Trying: The "Have a Go" Chart

Diane Smith, Kindergarten

"Oh, I love having a go at it," enthused Caroline as she spotted me flipping to the new chart page. With Erica beside her at the easel, she lifted the oak tag cover labeled "Have a go at it." Caroline and Erica were among the first kindergartners to get to the chart each day. They were confident of the letter sounds and frequently contributed to word spellings when we brainstormed as a group.

"Butadoes," Caroline said as she picked out matching green markers for herself and Erica. Today's pictured word was *potato*. They began to generate a spelling by stretching the word out and writing the letters of the sounds they heard.

"Buh, uh, da-a-a, do," Caroline said.

"No," Erica corrected, "*potato*'s a *P*. It's *P* in the *Vegetable ABC* book. I'll get it." She ran to the ABC book box, rifling through titles for a glimpse of the familiar cover. Cradling the book with both arms, she instructed, "I'll say it and you write it. *P-O-T-A-T-O*."

She handed the book to Caroline: "Now, you tell *me*." After she finished, they took turns signing their names under their respective work. Then both girls were off to the scrap box table, knowing work awaited them.

Noticing a vacancy at the easel, Jacob scrambled up from the rug, leaving behind his unfinished puzzle. Balancing on one knee, he slowly wrote JACOB, then glanced across the chart to where Caroline had written her attempt. Silently, he copied P-O-T-O from Caroline, omitting the A and the last O. Satisfied, he returned the marker to the tray. "I had a go," he bragged, skipping toward the block corner.

I remember the day when Kelly, our teacher-research group's facilitator, stopped by my classroom to ask what I thought of a passage in *Spelling in Use* (Laminack and Wood 1996) that describes a kindergarten classroom doing a "have a go" activity. This book was one of our research group's common readings.

Uh-oh, I thought, trying to remember what the book looked like. Should I go with "I don't think I have that one"? No, not with Kelly. "Actually, I'm not far into it," I said. "I forgot to bring it home over vacation." I only live a mile and a half from school, so I instantly regretted the second part of my lie.

Reading me, she answered, "It's only two or three pages. Here, I've tabbed it for you."

I smiled and lifted my eyebrows to acknowledge how pleased I was she had been thinking of me. In reality, I was less excited. Not anxious for more work, I located the tab, intending to scan the section quickly and get it off my desk so I could return to the business of filling out report cards. As she disappeared down the hall, I heard her say something about needing to know how useful I thought the activity might be.

When I turned to the tab, I found Laminack and Wood's description of how "have a go" works:

> During the class meeting on Monday morning in a kindergarten classroom, the teacher carefully uncovers a picture that has been taped or drawn on top of a large piece of chart paper. This morning, the picture is of an elephant. The teacher pronounces the word "*elephant.*" The children look at it carefully and immediately begin to think about it. These young writers know that sometime during the day they will come to this chart either alone or with a friend and generate a spelling for this word, *elephant.* (84–85)

Laminack and Wood went on to say that "This structure creates a *climate of trying* in the classroom" (86). I found this idea intriguing and immediately began to question my own practice. Had I provided enough opportunities to gently and naturally nudge my students toward writing those first words on their papers? I certainly made a point of letting them know how much I valued even those first tentative marks. I took advantage of every chance to model the process of stretching words out and writing down the names of letters we heard. Despite my efforts, however, few children managed to get much print on their papers during our daily ten-minute writing times. Even though more than half the class recognized all the letters and had a good grasp of the consonant sounds, they continued to concentrate mostly on their drawings. What was holding them back?

I recalled the dubious look on Marty's face just that morning when I had urged her to try writing just the first letter of each word in her "story." Together, we stretched the words out and isolated the first sound of each. "Last night I got new berjammies" became *L N I G N B.*

"You can *do* this, Marty," I assured her.

"But that's not what real spelling looks like," she protested.

And the children weren't the only ones who were concerned. One of my students' parents approached me on the playground while I was supervising late-bus students. Obviously upset, Mrs. Donnelly said, "Getting Brent out the door in the morning has been such a struggle lately. Last night he told my husband and I that you're making them write now. He's so worried about it. I told him that I would ask you if I could write the words of his story out and let him take the paper to class with him. He's good at copying words that his father and I write." Sensing my hesitation, she pleaded, "Or maybe you could tell us in advance what they will be writing about so that we can work on it at home?"

I quickly assured her that I certainly did not expect Brent to write like a grown-up and that I had repeatedly modeled listening for the letter sounds as the class and I stretched words out together. Defensively, I added that *any* mark on the story paper was given pretty significant attention. I went on to assert that any "play" at writing would move these beginning writers closer to those first real attempts at recording what they had to say. It was obvious from her expression that I had said little to reassure her.

"Sure, have him bring it with him tomorrow," I relented. There was no place for fear with five-year-old writers. Reluctantly, I admitted that Brent was probably not the only child who had worried himself sick about writing time. Something had to change. I had been expecting too much of these little ones, without providing the support they needed to be successful. I wondered if "have a go" might help bridge that gap.

I decided to introduce the "have a go" chart during our next morning meeting. Free Choice time, which followed our meetings, was nearly everyone's favorite part of the day. The children had forty-five minutes during which they could choose whatever they wanted to do. Every child had experienced success during Free Choice. Art, construction, dramatic play, snacks—few ideas were off limits if we could round up the supplies. "Have a go" would become another of the many options from which children could choose. And I knew markers and chart paper would be a big draw since those were usually the tools of the teacher.

Almost immediately, I could see that "have a go" did diffuse the risk of making a mistake. I was amazed at the high level of participation. Children were willing to wait in line so they could do their "have a go" first. A few took it as their job to round others up so they could fill as much of the chart as possible. If someone in the class happened to find the word written in a book or on a chart, it was big news, and it became the responsibility of our "detective" to make sure that everybody got a look at it. A few students would compare this new information to their attempt on the chart, but rarely did they feel a need to make changes. We found reasons to applaud any mark on the chart, and every child had a mark.

Attempts ranged from a child's name carefully printed in lowercase letters to a line of unsteady letters unrelated to sound. Some children copied a nearby attempt made by another child. Occasionally, I would watch as a child laboriously copied the name of a classmate, then signed his own name beneath it. Children who had more experience with print and knew something about correct form made a game of searching the room to find the word written somewhere. Those with little alphabet knowledge were frequently able to find the word themselves after it had been pointed out.

I gained insight into what strategies they relied on simply by observing as they interacted at the chart. Their conversations provided direction for future mini-lessons. Especially rewarding were the supportive comments they had for one another. Our third-grade reading partners also looked forward to "having a go" when they visited our classroom. I mistakenly assumed that the kindergartners would copy the older children's attempts, but my students again proved me wrong. They were proud of their work. "Trying" had become a worthwhile, reasonable goal.

As I have had time to reflect on the impact that simple activity had on my writing program, my own experiences as a learner have come into focus. Many, many times I have been every bit as reluctant as my young writers were to risk trying something new. I needed a climate for trying just as much as they did. How easy it is to overlook that critical step.

Conventional Wisdom and Common Ground: Inquiring About Spelling with Parents

Last spring, Gail did a workshop on spelling at a conference for Chapter I teachers, aides, and administrators. In a folder of handouts she prepared ahead of time, she included paper of various sizes, kinds, and colors. Her opening activity was to administer a brief list of tricky words, which she intended to use as a starting point for discussion about the strategies participants used as spellers. The most interesting aspect of the exercise, however, turned out to be the way the fifty members of the audience approached the task, not the strategies they used to figure out the words.

"When I told them I was going to give them a spelling test," Gail remembers, "everyone in the room automatically took the half-sheet of white lined paper out of their folders and started numbering to 20, without my telling them to do it. I stood back and watched. I smiled when I realized what they were doing. It was so telling about how ingrained our ideas about spelling are. It was an artifact of their past instruction."

We've found it helpful to keep this story in mind while thinking through our relationships with parents around spelling. As this anecdote reminds us, conventional wisdom surrounding spelling is strong, and much of the research on children's spelling development that discounts those assumptions is relatively recent, beginning with landmark studies by Charles Read (1971) and Carol Chomsky (1970) that have since been extended by Henderson and Beers (1980), Gentry (1982), Wilde (1992), and others. Since these findings had not widely influenced classroom practice when our students' parents were learning to read and write, most parents' spelling memories resemble Gail's workshop simulation far more than they resemble student-centered spelling investigations in Kim's fourth grade. We anticipated when we began our inquiry that we were likely to have some differences in perspective with parents, and we expected them to see spelling in more traditional terms than we did.

Even so, our experience as researchers in our classrooms had taught us to question easy assumptions, so eventually we began to wonder whether it made sense to see "The Parents" as an undifferentiated, anonymous group. We realized that we needed more specific information about our school community's beliefs and attitudes regarding spelling. Just because an audience of parents would probably respond to a test scenario using the same schema as the Chapter I personnel didn't necessarily mean that all of them saw these spelling norms as worth repeating. Did Mapleton parents want the same kind of instruction for their children that they had experienced? Could they envision other ways of teaching spelling? How did they think people learned to spell? And what kinds of activities were they pursuing as families that supported students' spelling development?

In order to answer these questions, we decided to gather data from families directly, rather than assume that we already knew the answers. In the remainder of this chapter, we'll tell you how we developed a spelling survey intended to enlist parents as partners in our inquiry, just as students had been. We'll describe some of the patterns we saw in the survey results, some of which were consistent with conventional wisdom and some of which challenged it. Then, we'll discuss how this new information affected both our work with students and our interactions with parents.

Although we are not experts on research design or analysis, we learned a great deal from writing and using a survey that we think can be useful to other teachers, whether you're simply polling your own students' parents or teaming up with other teachers to share your data. Since spelling is a topic of such concern to many parents, we strongly encourage you to solicit input from them if you are considering changes in your instruction.

Developing and Distributing the Surveys

Our survey was developed collaboratively during a research-group meeting. We announced the activity well ahead of time, so people could be thinking about items they wanted to include; then we recorded our brainstorming on several big pieces of chart paper. After a variety of possibilities had been raised, we discussed each of them in turn and decided exactly how we wanted to word each question, as well as sequence the entire series of questions.

Choosing which questions to include in the survey, and refining the language we used in them, forced us to articulate what kinds of information we wanted from parents, as well as to think about what we might do with that information. Our first concern was to eliminate any questions that might make respondents feel uncomfortable or exposed. For this reason, we decided not to ask parents whether they considered themselves or their children to be good spellers. Another question that we dropped from the list was the following: "Do you think good spelling is learned or inherited?" Although we were interested in what parents had to say about this issue, we couldn't see how their answers would affect our classroom practice in one way or another. We also decided against asking too many questions about how parents felt spelling should be taught in school because we couldn't necessarily commit to giving them the kinds of instruction many of them would request. We didn't want a large number of them to feel like their recommendations were dismissed or ignored if we couldn't act upon them.

After we had consensus on content, another consideration was how to format the survey so that it would be quick and simple for parents to complete, as well as easy for us to analyze the results. We decided that a combination of open-ended and closed responses would best serve our need for data we could easily summarize, as well as our desire to give parents a chance to speak out about spelling.

Since we felt that fine-tuning was most efficiently done by a small number of people, Kelly and Gail took the record of the group's ideas and constructed a first draft of the survey. Everyone received a copy to critique and edit before the final version was duplicated. Appendixes B–D include the survey that each of our 151 families received, along with a cover letter explaining our research and a release form allowing us to use children's work samples and photographs in publications or presentations.

In general, the packet went home with the oldest child in the family, although we made a few adjustments if Sharon O'Brien, our school secretary, felt that a younger sibling would be more reliable about returning the material. We requested that the surveys and release forms be returned within a week, which we judged as enough time for families to fill them out but not so much time they might get lost.

Ultimately, we received 126 surveys, representing about 83 percent of the total number of families served by the school. Our rate was undoubtedly

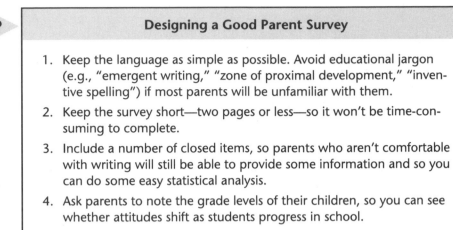

Designing a Good Parent Survey

1. Keep the language as simple as possible. Avoid educational jargon (e.g., "emergent writing," "zone of proximal development," "inventive spelling") if most parents will be unfamiliar with them.

2. Keep the survey short—two pages or less—so it won't be time-consuming to complete.

3. Include a number of closed items, so parents who aren't comfortable with writing will still be able to provide some information and so you can do some easy statistical analysis.

4. Ask parents to note the grade levels of their children, so you can see whether attitudes shift as students progress in school.

5. Include some room for parents to explain their answers if they choose to (some of our most interesting data came from these explanations).

6. Make including a name optional. Some parents will want to do so, and then they can be contacted for follow-up questions. Some will feel safer and be more honest if they can be anonymous.

7. Include a note that explains the purpose of the survey, so parents know why they should participate.

8. Explain to your students what you are doing and why so they can reinforce the survey's importance to their parents.

boosted by the fact that several teachers offered incentives to students whose families returned the survey. For example, Lorna gave lollipops to her fourth graders, and Gail rewarded returnees with fake money that could be used in the fifth grade's classroom economy. Although we were happy with this percentage, it probably would have been higher if we had sent the surveys home earlier in the year. We didn't get materials to parents until the end of May—a time of year when the school calendar and families' schedules are particularly busy.

Different members of our group participated in data analysis in different ways. At the retreat, everyone was able to close-read a set of twenty-five surveys and discuss them with a partner. Because we wanted to focus on trends in the parents' thinking as a group, not on figuring out which parent said what, each pair received a stack that represented a cross section of the whole batch, not just their "own" parents. As we read, we kept lists of patterns that we noticed and labeled interesting comments with tape flags, in order to share them during our whole-group discussion. Later, Vicky and Jill tabulated results for questions that generated numerical data, and Kelly coded parents' written responses using some of the categories we'd established in our first reading. Figure 4.1 includes a summary of these results.

Figure 4.1 Survey results for selected questions

Please note: Although 126 surveys were returned, not all parents chose to answer all questions.

1. How important do you feel spelling is? (124 responses)

not at all important				extremely important
1	2	3	4	5
0 (0%)	0 (0%)	8 (6.5%)	20 (16.1%)	96 (77.4%)

2. How do you think children become good spellers? (number in parentheses is the rank order of importance according to parents)

reading (1)	memorization (5)
natural ability (8)	studying words for tests (6)
workbook exercises (4)	using a dictionary (7)
breaking words into syllables (3)	writing (2)

5. How much time do you think should be spent on spelling in school? (121 responses)

20–30 minutes per day	61 (50.4%)
20–30 minutes per week	12 (9.9%)
no specific time; it should be incorporated into writing time	38 (31.4%)
other	10 (8.3%)

6a. Please circle the statement with which you most agree. (122 responses)

a. Children should receive a separate grade on their report cards for spelling.	85 (69.7%)
b. Spelling should be graded as a part of the writing process.	37 (30.3%)

6b. If you believe that children should receive a separate grade for spelling, at what level should that grading begin? (81 responses)

Grade 1: 30 (37.0%)
Grade 2: 22 (27.1%)
Grade 3: 21 (25.9%)
Grade 4: 5 (6.2%)
Grade 5: 3 (3.7%)

8. When is it important to spell correctly? (122 responses)

all the time	110 (90.2%)

Note: The 12 parents who did not check off "all the time" checked the following items:

when work is going to be publicly displayed	11
homework assignments	11
journals	0
on tests	9
other	4

What We Learned from Parents' Surveys

The following trends were prominent across the set of surveys we received.

Parents See Spelling as Critically Important

When Maine's learning standards were being developed with input from the public, parents across the state were asked to articulate their main hopes for their children's K–12 education. Of the ten most commonly cited goals, eight related to social and emotional development. Parents wanted their children to be able to work with others, to make healthy choices, and to be responsible citizens. Only two academic goals cracked the top ten: the ability to write clearly and the ability to spell correctly.

This same emphasis upon spelling was reflected among Mapleton parents who filled out our survey. Of the 124 people who responded to Question 1 ("How important do you feel spelling is?"), 77 percent selected 5, "extremely important," 16 percent selected 4; and 8 percent selected 3, "important." No one circled 1 or 2, the choices from the "not important" side of the continuum.

Written data from parents provided ample evidence of Bean and Bouffler's (1997) claim that "standard spelling has assumed an importance beyond the function it plays in written language. It has become the 'ticket' to the literacy club—the heir to the traditions and scholarly world of print" (67). For one parent, spelling mastery was crucial because it "can help them [students] go to a higher living life." Another felt that "You have to know it to get anywhere in life."

When parents were more specific about their reasons for the importance of spelling, their explanations generally fell into one of the following four categories:

- spelling's relationship to reading;
- the need for correctness in the job market and higher education;
- the negative effect on communication of inaccuracies;
- the way poor spelling reflects on individuals.

A sampling of quotations from each of these categories appears in Figure 4.2.

1. *Correct spelling is connected to better reading* (32%).

   "I feel spelling is the foundation to good reading, writing, and even pronunciation."
   "Spelling goes hand in hand with being a good reader. In order to do well in other subjects, a student needs to have good spelling and reading skills."
   "If a child does not know how to spell they can have problems learning to read."
   "Spelling teaches children to read and reading makes better people."

2. *Correct spelling will help students with jobs and higher education* (22%).

   "Spelling is used in every walk of life and every career. Whether you are writing a check or a note to your child's teacher or publishing a book it is very important."
   "Without the ability to spell and read as an adult it will be very difficult to compete for jobs or college."
   "Well if their [sic] graded on spelling at all throughout school (on book reports or any of their school work) learning spelling skills early on will definitely help. Also, as an adult, in my work and other facets of life, a good spelling background is a plus!"
   "Children need to know how to spell when filling out applications for jobs and further education facilities."

3. *Correct spelling aids communication* (19%).

   "If other people are going to be able to read their writings and understand it, the spelling needs to be accurate."
   "Vital for written communication."
   "Spelling is very important in communicating. Occasionally, a misspelled word can be misinterpreted and change the meaning of the message, causing miscommunication."
   "So people can read there [sic] writing."

4. *Correct spelling is a reflection upon the individual* (12%).

   "Accepting poor spelling at an early age gives the student just cause for the rest of their life—lazy spellers grow up to be lazy adult spellers which reflect's societies [sic] acceptance to be less than one ought to be."
   "Correct spelling allows good communication and is a form of self-respect. Our spelling represents us."
   "When you write something and it has misspelled (did I spell that word correctly?) words, it indicates to me you are not very knowledgeable so I don't take your content as seriously as I would otherwise."
   "I feel spelling is an important part of the way a person is perceived as being 'well educated.'"

Note: Numbers in parentheses represent the percentage of parents whose written explanation for their response to Question 1 ("How important do you feel spelling is?") fell in each of the four categories.

Figure 4.2 A sampling of reasons why Mapleton parents think spelling is important

Parents Want Time in School Devoted to Spelling Instruction

Fifty percent of our parents indicated that they felt twenty to thirty minutes per day was an appropriate amount of time for spelling. Another 18 percent favored separate time for spelling instruction, but in smaller increments; either they checked off "20–30 minutes per week" (10 percent) or they filled in another option under "other." For example, one mother suggested "1–2 hours/week—either in one whole time slot or so many minutes per day." Another parent, whose frustration with our program showed up in other areas of the survey, ended her statement that "Five or 10 minutes a day wouldn't hurt" with two exclamation points for emphasis. One father did note that the question was a difficult one to answer with a specific quantity of time for all children: "I would say whatever time it takes you to be a productive speller."

We were interested to see that a sizable minority of parents (31 percent) indicated that spelling should be incorporated into writing time. As one first grader's parent put it, "Writing and spelling kind of go together." Unfortunately, few of the other parents who checked this option offered any explanation of their choice, so we were unable to determine whether our message about spelling needing to be taught in the context of writing had influenced their decision.

Parents Think that People Should Spell Correctly All the Time

An amazing 90 percent of respondents checked this choice, with only 12 of 122 parents dissenting. We attribute this high percentage to several reasons. First of all, some parents' written comments suggested that they believed spelling errors in any writing context might "stick," causing students to make the same mistakes repeatedly. Parents also expressed concern that their children would become "lazy" or "sloppy" if there were times when they felt they didn't need to focus on spelling. These concerns seemed to be directly related to their beliefs, articulated in response to Question 1, that spelling was a "reflection of the individual." If poor spelling did reflect a lack of self-esteem, as one respondent argued, then it was not surprising that parents didn't want their children to indulge in it.

It is possible, however, that our check-off choices for Question 8 skewed our results, since our alternatives were limited to school writing tasks such as journals, tests, and homework assignments. We wonder whether parents' insistence on correctness would have carried through to such personal and informal genres as shopping lists, lecture notes, or written reminders to family members.

Parents Want to See a Grade in Spelling on Students' Report Cards

Although we struggled with our district report card's separate section for spelling (see Chapter 5 for more discussion of this issue), the responses to Question 6a suggested that most of our parents supported it. About 70 percent of the survey respondents felt that spelling should be graded as a discrete subject, rather than being subsumed beneath the broader heading of "writing." Presumably, they wanted to be able to monitor their children's progress closely in an area they felt was crucial. One parent even explained her answer with the following marginal comment: "They should know it [spelling] is as important as reading or writing."

It is worth noting, however, that nearly a third of our parents indicated a preference for spelling evaluation within the context of writing. In a number of cases, these were also the same parents who chose "no specific time; it should be incorporated into writing time" in response to Question 5, "How much time do you think should be spent on spelling in school?" One mother felt so strongly about the need for spelling to be taught and evaluated in the context of writing that she used six X marks to emphasize her choice for Question 5 and underlined her choice for Question 6a twice. In the margin next to both questions, she wrote, "Learning to spell just to pass a test *does not* work! I strongly feel it is learned through writing." Another parent expressed similar feelings next to the question on grading: "I don't agree with the weekly spelling words. I think they just memorize for the week to get an A on the test then forget about the words."

These comments and the number of respondents who expressed a preference for grading spelling in the context of writing reminded us of the diversity of opinions among our parents. They showed us that conventional wisdom is not impermeable and hinted that at least some parents had embraced the ideas we had introduced during conferences and open houses.

Parents Saw Reading and Writing as the Primary Ways Children Learn to Spell

One of the most striking findings of the survey was that most parents agreed with Frank Smith (1988)—and us!—that reading and writing are the most significant influences on learning to spell. Ninety-seven parents selected "reading" as their first or second choice for Question 2 ("How do you think children become good spellers?"), with sixty parents listing "writing" in one of the same two positions. By comparison, only eleven parents chose "memorization" and nine parents "studying words for tests" as one of their top two choices.

For us, these results were tremendously affirming, especially when we considered them in combination with the ways parents reported helping their children learn to spell at home (Question 3a). Although a number of parents did discuss traditional practices such as practicing oral drill, having their children copy their spelling words numerous times, and correcting their children's writing, far more of them talked about shared literacy activities that incorporated spelling in meaningful ways. Responses like the following were commonplace:

> "Reading, writing stories, working on the computer, making lists, reading grocery labels, etc."
>
> "First of all, we make *reading* a priority! We read every night at least one story. We take turns reading the pages. For spelling, we play games like hang-man or spelling bee—we get out the newspaper and take turns picking words to spell (it's fun)."
>
> "We play a game where I will spell the word 'it' and have her spell every word she knows using 'it'—then she gives me a word like 'at' and it's my turn. Sometimes I will make a mistake on purpose and see if she can catch it. We also play word games like Scrabble or Jumble."

Interestingly enough, some of the parents whose responses to other questions were most traditional (e.g., they wanted a big chunk of daily time devoted to spelling instruction and a separate grade for the subject) were the same parents who cited reading and writing as the most influential factors in spelling development and the same ones whose home practices were most in line with the things we would have recommended.

At first, we saw these results as contradictory and frustrating. We couldn't figure out why parents would recommend practices in one part of the survey whose effectiveness they discounted in other sections. After more consideration of the issue, however, we came to see these discrepancies as the perfect catalyst for conversation. If we could help parents value more highly the activities that worked for them at home—and then connect those activities explicitly to the factors that influenced spelling development—then perhaps they would be more supportive of similar endeavors in school.

What These Results Mean for Us (and Maybe You)

Before we discuss the concrete measures we took as a result of our data, we need to make it clear that it wasn't easy for us to face everything that parents said through the survey. Although most of the written comments we received were positive or neutral, there were a few exceptions. Given the opportunity to speak their minds about an issue of importance to them, a few survey respondents spoke bluntly—and sometimes antagonistically—about their distrust of our holistic methods. For example, one parent wrote, "It bugs me to see how little spelling my kids have in school. I could go on and on about this subject. What happened to the AEIOU and sometimes Y program?!"

Being a part of a group allowed us to process critical comments like these without feeling targeted as individuals. As we talked about the data, first in pairs and then as a large group, we were able to help each other look at the issues from multiple perspectives, rather than our own. These conversations led to new insights about parents and about ourselves as teachers. Lynne joked that confrontational parents would "do well to remember what my Mom used to say: 'You get more flies with honey than with vinegar,'" but her identification of a pattern in our data helped her be more sympathetic to parents' multiple points of view:

> I noticed that some of the parents who were most adamant about their feelings in favor of a structured program, tests, etc., were those who seem to struggle with spelling and good grammar themselves. I think they want better for their children and they're ready to fight for it. I guess I respect and admire that.

Lois realized that she needed to clarify her beliefs and expectations about spelling for herself because it was "scary" for her "to ask parents how they feel and what they want in and around an area where I don't feel completely confident myself." Once we were able to move beyond defensiveness and into this kind of reflection and analysis, the parent surveys became a catalyst for the spelling-focused initiatives described below.

The simplest way we could address parents' concerns was to take more care with the language we used to talk about spelling with them and with students. As a result, we decided to abandon terminology such as "sloppy copy" because we felt that it suggested a lack of concern for detail that the word *draft* does not connote. Instead of telling anxious student writers, "Don't worry about spelling—it doesn't matter yet," we resolved to use phrases like the following: "Spell the best you can right now, and we'll work on making it better when you edit." The second statement is only subtly different, we know, but we think it's less likely to be misinterpreted by parents who visit our classrooms or who receive our words secondhand, translated by their children. By speaking more precisely about our expectations regarding spelling, we can reassure parents that we value correctness—but not at the expense of more global goals such as clarity or fluency.

We also made a conscious effort to communicate more explicitly and more often about the specific ways we were addressing spelling in our classrooms. Instead of saying, "Spelling instruction takes place in the context of kids' writing," and leaving it at that, we learned to tell parents, in plain and simple language, about the "have a go" sheets that Judy's second graders filed in their folders to keep track of spellings they attempt. We also felt it was important to share with parents how we were approaching the kinds of skills and strategies addressed by published series. They needed to know that Lois's first graders were still studying spelling patterns on a regular basis; they were just doing it in the meaningful context of the morning message, rather than through a decontextualized list of twenty words. They needed to know that Martha's third graders learned about the different ways to spell /k/ through a discovery mini-lesson; they were just sorting the words and developing generalizations about the rules for themselves, rather than memorizing them. We resolved to write about these initiatives in our newsletters, to show artifacts that relate to them during conferences, and to highlight them during parent visits.

In addition to prompting more regular communication from individual classrooms, our analysis of the survey data pushed us to develop a schoolwide belief statement about spelling that could then be shared with parents. Charged with keeping the statement brief and jargon-free, several members generated a draft, which we then discussed as an entire group. After we came to consensus on both the content and the wording, Gail introduced the document to the parents in a letter from the principal:

Belief Statement About Spelling—Mapleton Elementary School

1. Spelling is a problem-solving activity, not a simple matter of memorization and drill. Children must be provided with opportunities to develop their own understandings of how the spelling system works.
2. Spelling is a tool for communication, not an end in itself.
3. Opportunities to do a great deal of reading and writing for meaningful purposes are necessary, though not sufficient, conditions for learning to spell.
4. Some children are naturally better spellers than others, but all students can and should learn to edit their writing to correctness.
5. The ability to spell well is not a measure of intelligence, nor does its lack automatically reflect laziness or carelessness.
6. Teachers' and parents' high but reasonable expectations for spelling help children achieve correctness in their writing.

Gail also included a summary of the survey results and the steps we had taken because of these results. In this way, we hoped to communicate to parents that their input had been taken seriously, leading to concrete action on our part.

It was clear from the surveys that many parents spent a great deal of time helping their children with spelling at home. As Judy pointed out, "Studying with their children seems to give a purpose to parent involvement. It's something they know how to do." As we read through answers to Question 3a ("What do you do at home to help your child be a better speller?") that focused on drill, we realized that we needed to develop and disseminate a list of other ways that parents could help their children grow as spellers. If we weren't going to encourage parents in their familiar role as the coach for weekly spelling tests, then we needed to suggest some alternatives. Fortunately, the alternatives didn't need to come just from us: They could be gleaned from the surveys themselves, since numerous parents had written about ideas that were well worth sharing with others. The Tip on the next page, "Ways Parents Can Help with Spelling at Home," contains the list of at-home possibilities that a small group of us generated.

We also needed to rethink how parent volunteers might help with spelling in the classroom. A number of members of our group had developed a rich tradition of assistance from parents. In Judy's second grade, for

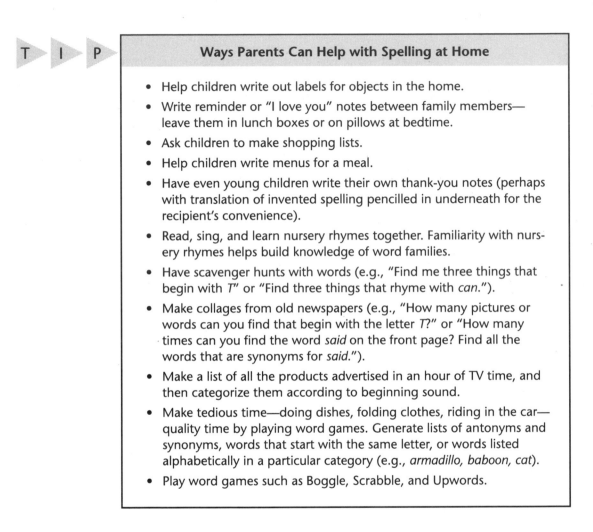

T ▷ I ▷ P

Ways Parents Can Help with Spelling at Home

- Help children write out labels for objects in the home.
- Write reminder or "I love you" notes between family members—leave them in lunch boxes or on pillows at bedtime.
- Ask children to make shopping lists.
- Help children write menus for a meal.
- Have even young children write their own thank-you notes (perhaps with translation of invented spelling pencilled in underneath for the recipient's convenience).
- Read, sing, and learn nursery rhymes together. Familiarity with nursery rhymes helps build knowledge of word families.
- Have scavenger hunts with words (e.g., "Find me three things that begin with *T*" or "Find three things that rhyme with *can*.").
- Make collages from old newspapers (e.g., "How many pictures or words can you find that begin with the letter *T*?" or "How many times can you find the word *said* on the front page? Find all the words that are synonyms for *said*.").
- Make a list of all the products advertised in an hour of TV time, and then categorize them according to beginning sound.
- Make tedious time—doing dishes, folding clothes, riding in the car—quality time by playing word games. Generate lists of antonyms and synonyms, words that start with the same letter, or words listed alphabetically in a particular category (e.g., *armadillo, baboon, cat*).
- Play word games such as Boggle, Scrabble, and Upwords.

example, parents administered word lists to students, graded the tests, and recorded their scores. It was a clearly defined way for them to participate in the classroom, and many of them did so with a good deal of pride and commitment. As we moved away from weekly testing, though, we needed to find some alternatives so parents' participation could continue. Below are some other ways parent volunteers might contribute to students' spelling development:

- interviewing students about their spelling attitudes (see Figure 2.1 for a sample) and recording their answers

- helping small groups of children generate lists of words with a common factor (e.g., the same beginning sound or different ways to spell the ending /shun/)
- monitoring students' personal spelling lists to make sure the entries are spelled correctly and to see whether students have mastered them
- determining the index of control for pieces of students' writing (see "Determining an Index of Control," p. 114)
- editing students' writing with them—guiding children in using the computer spellcheck correctly, in using a dictionary, or in "having another go" (see the Interlude "Having a Go at Spelling Strategies") with words they're not sure of

Some of these suggestions may require a bit more orientation and/or training than administering and correcting tests, but we think they're manageable for parents and meaningful for student spellers.

We further explored some of these possibilities for parent involvement at home and at school when we hosted a mini-conference in November of 1998 for parents and area educators. If you're like most teachers and don't have the resources (or necessarily the desire!) to sponsor a conference, you might consider hosting a Family Spelling Night instead. We suggest modeling the evening on a Berkeley-developed vision for Family Math Night (Stenmark, Thompson, and Cossey 1986), where parents and children gather together at school to participate in hands-on, curriculum-related activities in a relaxed, informal atmosphere. You might ask attendees to sort words and develop generalizations, to do some collaborative writing and editing, or to share some of their favorite tricks for remembering challenging words. In this way, parents can get a flavor for what research-based spelling instruction feels like in a progressive classroom, which may help them let go of some of their conventional wisdom.

Our last, and perhaps most important, insight from the data was one not so easily addressed with a concrete strategy like the publishing of a list or the dissemination of a newsletter. Many of the open-ended responses to the survey suggested that we needed to help parents see spelling in a broader context of reading and writing. The surveys suggested that approximately a third of our parents saw spelling as a "gatekeeper" to reading—not as a set of skills that develop more fully as students garner more experience as readers and writers. Although we thought we'd helped most of our students' parents to move beyond a "bottom-up," decoding-first conception of reading, their attitudes about spelling revealed the fault lines in their thinking. Many of them believed spelling to be crucial because it helped unlock the secrets of reading, letter by letter, sound by sound. They had embraced our message that reading, writing, and spelling are interconnected processes, but they didn't see the relationships, or the sequence of development, in the same way we did.

In a similar vein was the parents' overwhelming consensus (90 percent) that it was important to spell correctly all the time. This wasn't just a statement about spelling: it reflected a philosophy of writing that, unlike ours, didn't take context into consideration. It indicated to us that not only did we need to demonstrate the predictable patterns of spelling development more clearly and concretely, but we also needed to help both students and parents think in more sophisticated ways about purpose and audience and the roles they play in the composing process, as well as the ways they influence our emphasis on correctness. We needed to communicate why we had one set of expectations for the amount of energy that should be expended on a grocery list, and another set for a college essay or a letter to a newspaper editor. Because we had come to see spelling as a problem-solving activity, not merely a mechanistic skill or habit, we believed that student writers could learn to make the same distinctions for themselves.

Looking to the Future

Helping the members of our school community come to deeper, more data-driven understandings about literacy is a challenging task. It won't happen overnight, and it won't happen without a good deal of effort on our part. We know now that we can't expect an occasional newsletter and a yearly conference to help parents assimilate new research on spelling development into their thinking. We need to be patient, to keep chipping away at conventional wisdom while trusting the insights we have gained from closely observing children at work.

At the same time, our survey data demonstrated the importance of finding some common ground with our parents about the teaching and learning of spelling. We need to respect where parents are coming from and to address their concerns explicitly. Ultimately, they may be more closely connected to "real-world" attitudes about spelling than we are (they certainly represent a more heterogeneous population than we do!), and we want our students' work to stand up to the challenges of that real world. Our research and reading have convinced us that we don't need to return to word lists and weekly tests to accomplish the goals we share with parents; now it's up to us to share that message in multiple ways.

A closing note: Although we hope these survey results and our responses to them are informative for other teachers, we want to stress that our sample of parents was a small one, and our results are rooted in a particular context, at a particular time. For these reasons, we highly recommend that you gather data about spelling from parents in *your* community. We hope the following Extensions will help you be successful if you choose to do so.

Extensions

1. Using some of the tips outlined in this chapter, develop a survey or questionnaire for parents regarding their beliefs about spelling. You may want to enlist a colleague or a group of colleagues to help you generate and refine your questions, or better yet, see if others are interested in sharing their data and looking for patterns together.
2. Complete your own survey before you pass it along to parents. In this way, you may be able to pinpoint any ambiguities in your questions. Perhaps more important, you'll have a chance to make your own beliefs about spelling explicit, which may make it easier to avoid the pitfall of unintentionally evaluating each parent's response against your own vaguely articulated ideal answers.
3. Field-test your survey with a small number of parents before sending it to the target group in general. Getting their input may help you improve the clarity and respectfulness of the questions. You may also be able to use the survey as the starting point for an in-depth interview with a selected group of parents.
4. Help students develop a series of interview questions for their parents about their attitudes toward and experiences with spelling. Not only will this activity generate data for you to consider, but it may also prompt interesting conversations between children and their parents. After the interviews are completed, you and the children can discuss how to represent and analyze the data, which may lead you to incorporate math skills and visual thinking into the activity as well.

INTERLUDE

Having a Go at Spelling Strategies

LORNA TOBIN, GRADE 4

It was the same old question that I faced at the start of every new school year: "What am I going to do about spelling?" I would search through issues of *Mailbox*, looking for the spelling cure, anything that would keep me away from the weekly spelling tradition of word lists. I had done these before, sometimes even allowing students to choose their own words, but my frustration escalated when the kids continued to misspell them in their daily writing. I was confident that they were immersed in a variety of meaningful reading and writing experiences, but something was missing.

Determined to solve this dilemma, I began reading professionally. *Invitations* (Routman 1994) became my Bible study, and I realized that my spelling program lacked an important component: a way to help students develop the strategies they needed to become better spellers. The more I read about "have a go" sheets, the more I thought they might be helpful for strategy building. Students would have a chance to identify words from their writing that were misspelled and to make multiple attempts at correcting them—both of which were strategies used by proficient adult writers.

I decided to introduce the idea to my fourth graders. After I gave them all a copy of the "have a go" sheet, I talked about how they were going to use it for words that they were misspelling often in their writing. They needed to choose important words, words that they used all the time, but they were only going to choose five per week to work on (see Figure 4.3 for a completed example from a student named Kathy). In the past, when students picked their own words for spelling, I had asked for ten words a week, and it was too many. The smaller number of words they had, the better. We would zero in on those five words, and that would be enough for them to handle.

Initially, they chose their five words from their writing folders, journals, or their bookmarks—half-sheets of paper they completed with thoughtful comments after they finished reading a book. All of these writing tasks included misspelled words that were important to them and part of their vocabularies.

Students had a set time to work on their "have a go" sheets once or twice a week for about thirty minutes, and I was available to help them indi-

HAVE A GO

Kathy

	Invented Spelling	1st Attempt	2nd Attempt	Standard Spelling
3/6/98	becouse	becoues	becouse	because
	sould	should		should
	hapen	happen		happen
	usto	useto	uston	used to
	seams	seems		seems
3/10/98	sposto	suposto	supostureo	suppose to
	ether	either		either
	coson	cusin	casion	cousion
	ider	idus	idea	idea
	berries	berrays	berries	berries
3/20/98	under-stud	under-stoud	under-stood	understood
	wally	usaly	ussially	usually
	carekter	charikter	coreickter	character
	varye	very		very
	intereced	interested	interested	interested
3/30/98	stenchen	attenchen	attenchan	attention
	fellt	felt		felt
	died	dyed		died
	spashal	speshel	speshal	special
	subtrck	subtraek	subtrack	subtract
4/13/99	sceuos	cekual	sekuool	sequal
	tuck	take		take

Figure 4.3 A sample "have a go" sheet from Kathy, a fourth grader

vidually. I learned quite a bit about them when I circulated. I'd try to help some of them with their second attempts if I thought they were having a really hard time. I also began placing dots under the letters that were correct in a particular word, so they could focus on the part that wasn't correct. Kids responded favorably to this strategy. Some of them would actually come to me and ask, "Would you dot my words for me?" This happened most often when they were on a first attempt and didn't know where to go from there. I wondered if they hadn't learned enough about spelling strategies to take them to that next step.

As I observed students at work over time I noticed that many of them were just trying to take a word through two or three steps by rearranging the letters and trying to eyeball it. Some of them were going straight to the dictionary, not knowing what else to do. While these were certainly important strategies to try, I realized then that I was expecting students to make several attempts at a word with a very limited sense of other options they could use to change it. So I called the kids together for a class meeting and said, "What do you do when you're trying to spell a word you don't know?" They came up with pretty basic strategies: go to the dictionary, ask someone else, ask the teacher, and sound it out.

That's when I decided to spend more time doing directed mini-lessons, not just working with students one on one. I set aside a time to do this, usually ten to fifteen minutes before they started working independently. I had already looked at their sheets and seen evidence of patterns. Those patterns would lead to a lesson on how they might use a particular rule. We would talk about some of the words they were missing. I would put those words on the board and ask, "Can you see a pattern among these words? Can you see what's happening with all of them?" When they said yes, we would talk about a spelling rule that applied. I might say, "See if this can help you the next time you come to a word that should have a double consonant."

I also took back some of the control in selecting their individualized lists for the week. I wanted to make sure they were choosing words that would transfer to other writing situations. Bookmarks were a good source of words for "have a go" because students used some of the same language from week to week; words such as *beginning, favorite, excellent,* and *detailed* were repeatedly misspelled. I would look through their bookmarks and find five words apiece that I felt they should be spelling correctly in fourth grade. I would write these words on a Post-it as they were spelled (see Figure 4.4). Then the students would transfer the words to their "have a go" sheets and work through several attempts using whatever strategies they had.

As we kept doing this, students would pass their bookmarks in, and I had a harder time finding misspellings. Words like *enjoyed* were not spelled *enjoied* anymore. I brought this up in class one day: "I don't see many misspelled words on your bookmarks anymore." One of the students raised his hand and said, "We don't want to get Post-its on our bookmarks." It made

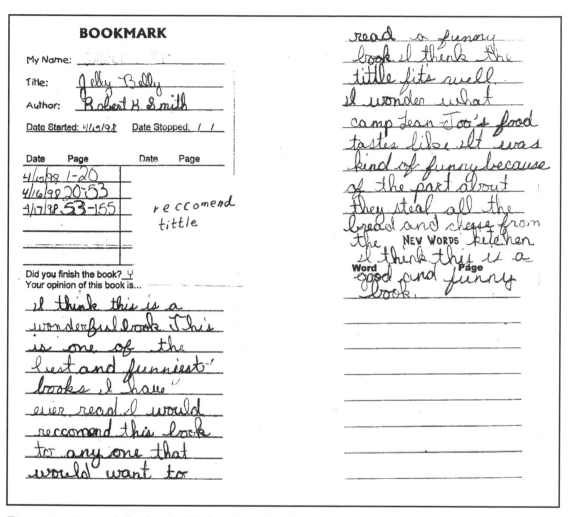

Figure 4.4 A sample bookmark filled out by a fourth grader

me feel a little guilty, but then I thought, "It's making them more aware of the importance of those words on the bookmarks, and they need those words to write about books." I didn't feel it was affecting the way they expressed themselves or inhibiting their word choices. I paid closer attention when I was passing the bookmarks out, and I could hear them chatting: "I only have two words on my Post-it this time." They were glad about having a concrete way for them to measure their improvement.

I was also able to return some of the responsibility for choosing words to the students. If I only found one or two misspellings on their bookmarks, then they could go to their writing folders or their journals to find three or four words on their own to make their limit of five. At that point, they were beginning to choose words that were critical to their editing.

I continued to observe how students worked on their sheets. Some of the kids liked to have dots put beneath the correct letters of tricky words, so they enlisted each other to do that for them. They knew who the good spellers in the room were, and they often asked those peers for help in checking their words or getting enough letters right to use the dictionary. There was a lot of rich talk at their tables about the words they had on their Post-its and the ones they had chosen themselves.

At the end of the year, I held a class meeting to talk about whether students felt the "have a go" sheets had helped them. I wrote down what they said on a chart, and a student recorded their comments on a piece of paper so I could refer to it more easily. "They showed us what words we needed to work on," one boy said. Several students mentioned using the rules we talked about in class meetings to check their spelling after writing a rough draft. Laura talked about taking a notepad and using that little piece of paper to spell words on her own while she was drafting; she had really internalized that strategy. Justin had written himself a note—"Spell it right the first time"—on the back of his sheet after I did a mini-lesson on "one-second words" (Wilde 1997), words they could spell correctly on their own if they took just one second to think about them. For him, the "have a go" sheet was a place to consolidate his resources about spelling. A number of students also used the sheet as a resource during writing time. It was a point of reference for them, a place where they knew they had certain words spelled correctly.

Another interesting piece of data came from the portfolio conference evaluations that students wrote in June. Most of the words in Laura's reflection (Figure 4.5) were spelled correctly, even though she'd struggled with spelling at the beginning of the year. I was particularly happy to see that she had conventional spellings for words like *favorite* and *imaginary* that she had worked through on her "have a go" sheet.

This year, I'm using "have a go" sheets again, but I'm being more deliberate about how we start out. I don't think I gave students enough information last year, so now I'm using an overhead to model more carefully the steps of going through multiple attempts and checking them. I also started with a conversation and chart about what strategies they were familiar with. We're keeping that chart visible and adding to it every time we learn a new strategy.

PORTFOLIO CONFERENCE EVALUATION

Name _Laura_   Date _6-8-98_

Comments: Reading	Comments: Writing
I can Read alot of books. books can help you learn lots of things and take you on a imoginory adventure. I love too Read it is my favorite Subject Reading can help you become a better speller. Because when you look or see a word alot you will see the shapes or form of that word and it will stick in your hed	I can Edit my draft I dont go to the dictionary rough away I try to spell the word and then look for it I sometimes break the word into Scellable or sound it out

Goals: Reading	Goals: Writing
1. to read more book and to be able to read harder books	1. To be able to spell better and write neata

Figure 4.5 Self-evaluation by Laura, a fourth grader

Farewell to the EZ Grader: Inquiring About Spelling Assessment and Evaluation

When Enola began teaching first grade in 1975, she was working in a school where she was expected to give spelling tests. "That was okay—I could do that," she remembers, "but when it came to actually grading the tests themselves . . . I could not bring myself to call a whole word wrong if the child had just missed one or two letters. So I would count up all the letters in the list of spelling words, get out my EZ Grader, and only deduct points for the missed letters."

We laughed when Enola told us this story at a research-group meeting, but it rang true in a serious way, too. As uncomfortable as many of us were about teaching spelling in a traditional way, we were even more so about *evaluating* spelling using that paradigm. We had the same questions Enola did: How can I avoid demoralizing students who struggle? How can I show that I value students' attempts, even if they're not correct? How can I give credit to students for good habits and strategies? We knew that sixteen words spelled correctly on a weekly spelling test of twenty words didn't mean that a particular student could spell correctly 80 percent of the time in her writing; nor did it mean that the child would be able to spell those same words correctly the following week.

When our inquiry began, we were just as uncomfortable with our report card because, like teachers in many school districts, we were required to record a quarterly spelling mark for students in grades 2 through 5. This mandate was a historical source of tension for us for two reasons. First, we had philosophical objections to separating spelling from the writing process.

Like Sandra Wilde (1992), we felt that assigning a grade for spelling outside the context of writing was much like giving kids separate grades for math and for multiplication. Although we felt that spelling deserved considerable attention, we did not want to suggest with our evaluation tools that it was just as important as reading and writing.

In addition, we had practical concerns about how to determine these grades fairly and consistently. When they were based primarily on spelling test scores, they did not always reflect students' performance in other contexts. Some children diligently studied their weekly spelling lists and made excellent grades on tests, yet their spelling in written work continued to be erratic. Other children were good natural spellers who performed well on both standardized and teacher-made tests but made little effort to learn new words or check their writing. Should they receive a higher grade than students who worked hard at editing their work but made more mistakes than their peers? How much did improvement count? Although few of us chose to tackle these questions directly, we couldn't help bumping up against them as we pursued inquiry questions such as "What happens when fourth graders select interesting words for a weekly spelling meeting?" and "What spelling strategies do emergent writers demonstrate during editing conferences?"

We might never have realized how much thinking we'd actually done about assessment and evaluation if Gail and Martha hadn't found *Spelling: From Beginnings to Independence* (Department for Education and Children's Services [DECS] 1997) at a conference they attended in Chicago. According to this resource guide, a good spelling evaluation program has three components—observation, conferencing, and product analysis—with both teacher evaluation and student self-evaluation occurring in each category (43).

As we talked about this framework, we realized we'd already been using it; the resemblance between the DECS categories and the kinds of data we collected for our inquiry was striking. Although our original goal for our research was to improve our spelling instruction, the work led to another unintended benefit: Analyzing data from our classrooms helped us become better assessors and evaluators of students' spelling—almost without our noticing it. We think classroom-based inquiry can do the same thing for you, and we'd argue that it's easier (and also more pleasant) to develop your skills in this indirect way, while focusing on broader questions of interest to you, than it is to tackle assessment and evaluation directly at a time when those issues are often fraught with tension and conflict. As we see it, classroom-based inquiry and good evaluation practices have a number of similarities. Both are:

- guided by questions about what students know and need to know
- based on analysis of data
- intended to determine next steps for better instruction
- most effective when students are involved in the process
- intended to generate results that can then be shared with other interested parties

The remainder of this chapter is not intended to provide an exhaustive blueprint for a spelling evaluation program. We haven't included more than a few sample tools (if you'd like to see some other examples, you might investigate some of the resources we recommend in Appendix A), and we have not tracked a single student's spelling through multiple drafts as is customary in many professional books on spelling. Instead, we've decided to use the three-part DECS schema as a way to frame our discussion of the spelling assessment and evaluation strategies that were most consistent with our emphasis on inquiry for both students and teachers. As you might expect, very few of these examples fall cleanly into one category or another, which means that one teacher's initiative may rely on more than one source of data—mostly observation plus a little bit of product analysis, for instance. Given the complexity of learning to spell, we think this is appropriate. At the end of the chapter, we'll describe how these mostly formative evaluation practices nudged us to develop a new summative evaluation tool: a school-wide rubric for spelling.

Observation

The DECS framework presents observations as a way for teachers to see how student spellers use spelling resources, collaborate with each other, and apply information from instruction and modeling. Although we have been committed kidwatchers (Goodman 1978) since our adoption of a holistic language arts philosophy in the late 1980s (see Chapter 1), we were not always systematic or deliberate about watching kids spell. In fact, before we began our inquiry, our anecdotal records were more likely to include information about students' topic choices, fluency, and willingness to share their pieces than they were to address students' self-corrections, use of visual strategies, or awareness of syllabification. With our adoption of a teacher-research stance, we began to pay closer attention to the latter kinds of data, and to document them more carefully.

These observations frequently helped us get a handle on where individual students were coming from and determine directions for writing conferences. If enough students seemed to be struggling with the same issue—such as how to represent middle sounds of a word by stretching it out—then we might plan a whole-group mini-lesson on that topic.

Careful observations also helped some of us decide what *not* to teach. For example, after hearing Martha talk about her third graders' difficulty with dictionary guide words (see Chapter 3), Gail wanted to determine her fifth graders' proficiency with the same skill. She gathered enough dictionaries so every child in the class would have one, and then she dictated a list of words, one by one, for students to locate as quickly as possible. Nearly every child in the class was able to do this swiftly and accurately. When students shared page numbers for the words, Gail asked them to articulate the strategies they used to find them—something at which they were equally adept. At the end of this twenty-minute activity, Gail was able to talk over what she noticed with Vicky, her instructional aide, who had been taking detailed notes. Both sets of observations demonstrated that further instruction in using guide words was unnecessary for the fifth graders.

Observations also helped Lois, who was charting word patterns in conjunction with the morning message, to nudge her first graders toward greater spelling growth. Initially, each day one student chose a word for the class to explore, and then another student decided what the group might do with it. As time went on, Lois noticed that students almost always chose to generate a list of words beginning with the same sound as the one they pulled from the message (e.g., the word *basketball* might kindle a list of *b*-words such as *boy, bag,* and *bite*). Since most of the children had already become proficient at representing the initial sound of the words they wanted to write, these lists weren't helping them come to new understandings about spelling.

In order to "up the ante," Lois made a new rule that initial sounds were off-limits—an intervention that forced the children to consider different kinds of patterns that related more squarely to spelling challenges they faced as writers (e.g., rhyming words, words with a particular ending such as *-er*, or compound words). At the same time the children were engaged in finding patterns in words, Lois was looking for patterns in their behavior that would lead her to make crucial adjustments to her practice.

We found that data from observations provided a good starting point for a number of other evaluation strategies. Without being intrusive, we could watch students at work and formulate some questions about their intentions or their grasp of a particular concept. Our initial impressions could be checked against other sources of data by administering a word list, examining a piece of writing, or pulling a chair alongside a student's desk for a conference.

Conferencing

According to the DECS framework, conferencing about spelling enables teachers to do the following:

- assess a student's needs and plan for specific teaching and learning;
- give students feedback on their achievement;
- help students plan for spelling improvement. (47)

When we began our inquiry project, nearly all of us were comfortable with individual writing conferences as a way to accomplish these goals in a meaningful context. Conferring over a student's draft allowed us to determine both what the child knew and what he or she needed to know next, and it was probably the most commonly used spelling assessment technique in our building. As we were drawn deeper into our research, we continued to use and refine this method, but we also discovered several other kinds of conferences that could enhance our assessment and evaluation of students' spelling.

First of all, we learned that spelling conferences didn't always have to start with a written draft as the catalyst. For example, Lorna had a highly effective conference with Lisa, one of her fourth graders, that began with the "have a go" sheet Lisa was keeping of misspelled words from her writing. A pattern in the initial misspellings recorded in the first column of the sheet suggested to Lorna that her student struggled with blends. In words like *tried*, *spoke*, and *subtract*, Lisa was consistently omitting or misplacing the second consonant. When Lorna knelt by Lisa's desk to discuss these observations, she was able to confirm her hunch: Lisa was not familiar with the term "blend," and she did not realize that there was a common thread among many of the words she wrote incorrectly. After a brief explanation of the concept, Lorna made a list of common blends in the margin of Lisa's "have a go" sheet that could serve as a resource for her when spelling future words beginning with blends. Lorna's later conferences with Lisa, as well as checks of her "have a go" sheets, showed significant improvement in this area.

We also learned that the children weren't the only ones who could benefit from conferencing: Their parents could, too. Diane used her conference time as a way to inform parents about the kindergartners' daily attempts to "have a go" at spelling pictured words. Because this activity was available to the children during choice time—a part of the day when students were playing, talking, or reading with a minimum of intervention from her—Diane was able to hear how individual children stretched out the sounds in the word and consulted with each other about how to represent them. She could watch them consult books in the reading corner and charts on the wall—decisions that indicated how much they were attending to print in their environment.

When conferences rolled around, Diane was able to share this observational data. By referring to specific contributions to the "have a go" charts, she was able to demonstrate to parents that their children knew a good deal about how words work, even if they were not ready to spell them conventionally. On a single chart, parents could see attempts representing different levels of spelling development; across the charts, they could see growth in their individual child's work. According to Diane, the parents' questions and anxiety about invented spelling decreased noticeably after these conferences.

Gail, Kelly, and Martha also discovered another tool that could be used in conjunction with conferencing: the developmental feature list (Hughes and Searle 1997). Ranging in difficulty from *rag* to *condemnation*, the eighty-four words on the list were carefully chosen because their spellings would demonstrate whether children controlled such features as letter doubling, adverbial endings, and prefixes (see the Tip "A Developmental Feature List" on the next page). Like a miscue analysis or a running record in reading, the list is intended to elicit errors; without them, no window is gained on students' use of strategies and problem solving. Although it's certainly possible to dictate a number of these words for an entire class to spell, this is not how we used the list, nor what its developers advocate. Instead, we encourage you to use it as a basis for an individual or small-group conference so that you will be able to watch students closely and ask them to articulate what decisions they are making as they spell. While this method is more time-consuming than the traditional one, we found that the payoff was significantly greater in terms of usable knowledge about students' strengths and weaknesses.

Not only did the developmental feature list offer us the chance to assess students' strategy use in action, but it also provided opportunities for on-the-spot intervention based upon the data we collected. For example, when Kelly asked a small group of fifth graders to spell a selection of words from

T ▶ I ▶ P ▶

A Developmental Feature List

For more details on how to use the feature list, we refer you to Hughes and Searle's (1997) book *The Violent E and Other Tricky Sounds: Learning to Spell from Kindergarten Through Grade 6.*

rag	shock	sign	invite
six	stained	signal	invitation
game	trained	please	exception
nice	chirped	pleasant	attract
yellow	jumped	pleasure	attractive
kiss	learned	knowledge	attraction
hill	chick	city	grocery
muffin	shed	cities	groceries
back	puppy	compete	terror
hero	puppies	competition	terrify
camp	geese	nerve	terrified
doctor	year	nervous	acknowledge
drive	exciting	rejoice	usual
yell	excuse	beauty	usually
pickle	know	beautiful	connect
quick	knife	beautifully	connection
late	eagle	special	responsible
once	teacher	featuring	irresponsible
butter	feature	probable	irresponsibility
batter	brave	improbable	condemn
wife	bravely	probably	condemnation

the list, she discovered that the students were troubled by vowels in the middle of long words. All of the students misspelled *invitation* and *competition* on the first try, with three out of four spelling the second syllable of both words with an *a* rather than the correct vowel:

MARTY:	compatetion	invatation
PETE:	compatition	invatation
RACHEL:	compatison	invataion
CHRISTINA:	compateshion	invatashon

Since the students' misspellings involved a schwa—a weak vowel sound occurring in unaccented syllables that can be represented by *a, e, i, o,* or *u*—students could not rely on sound to help them determine the correct spelling. Instead, they needed to use meaning cues—something they didn't appear from their conversation to be activating. When Kelly asked them to spell the verb forms of both words (*invite* and *compete*), a strategy she hoped would remind them of the semantic relationships between the words, Marty and Pete were able to use that information to correct both of the longer words. Thus, the conference over the developmental feature list shifted seamlessly from a data-collection method to a vehicle for carefully targeted instruction that made an immediate difference for several students.

Finally, we learned that conferences provided opportunities for teachers' learning as much as for students'. Rather than keeping a separate file of conference documentation, Gail found it useful to write a few notes directly on the student's rough draft. She recorded bits of the student's conversation with her, as well as any skills she had taught or reinforced. This strategy worked particularly well during a recent meeting with Terence, one of her fifth graders, about a story he had written on snowboarding that included sentences such as "I am comeing down the hill" and "I am raceing through the snow."

"I made a list of verbs from his story like the following: *come/coming, race/racing, wait/waiting,*" Gail writes. "He quickly generated the rule and then corrected the spelling." Throughout the lesson, Gail kept notes about the conversation on Terence's rough draft, and the annotated piece was filed in his folder. Not only were these notes a reference for Terence and documentation for Gail, but they also served as a potential resource for another child in the class: "If someone else has the same problem, I can send them to Terence for help, and he has the tracks of the mini-lesson to work from."

This incident also illustrates the value of taking a teacher-research stance to conferences. According to Gail,

> This was a simple little one-paragraph story. It won't win any literary awards—probably wouldn't even be a piece you would select for a portfolio. But talk about evidence of learning about writing! I was reminded of some very important matters today. Terence was trying to capture a single event, not write a story. He wanted to write in present tense so it would "be more exciting." He knew what he wanted to do but could not label it. If he hadn't insisted on using present tense, I would not have had this opportunity. Instead of *comeing, raceing,* and *waiting,* here's the pattern I would have seen instead:

came
raced
waited

Looking at this snippet of my day as a teacher-researcher made the difference. Terence learned a skill, but I learned much more.

Product Analysis

Like the South Australian DECS, we valued product analysis because it allowed us to see students' strategy use in action and track their progress over time. Each of us was experienced in this kind of analysis because for years we had conducted daily conferences with students as part of writers' workshop. We learned to take our appraisal of student samples to a new level, however, by discussing them during our research-group meetings. Our attention to patterns and our appreciation of subtle evidence of growth increased, in addition to several other insights.

First, we learned that product analysis is often more complex when multiple perspectives are included. During our summer retreat, we spent a chunk of time examining writing in response to the schoolwide prompt we adopted (see Chapter 2). Some of our most fruitful insights came when we analyzed samples that did not come from our grade level. When Lynne, a first-grade teacher, and Gail, a fifth-grade teacher and the school's teaching principal, conferred over a piece from fourth grader Joe Jenkins (Figure 5.1), their collaboration enabled them to come to complex understandings about his spelling. Working from the positively framed question "What does this student know about spelling?" they generated the following insights regarding Joe's writing about a special person, his dad:

- Although eight of the more than 80 words in the piece were misspelled, all of them were close enough approximations (e.g., *bom* for *bomb*, *polis* for *polish*) that meaning was not lost for the reader.
- Several of his misspellings (e.g., *spacila, exampel*) included all or nearly all of the right letters, but the order was mixed up. Joe's move from *spaical* (first draft) to *spacila* (second draft) suggests that he knew that the letter *c* needed to be followed by an *i* in this case to be soft.
- He was able to spell *because,* a difficult word for most fourth graders, correctly in both drafts.

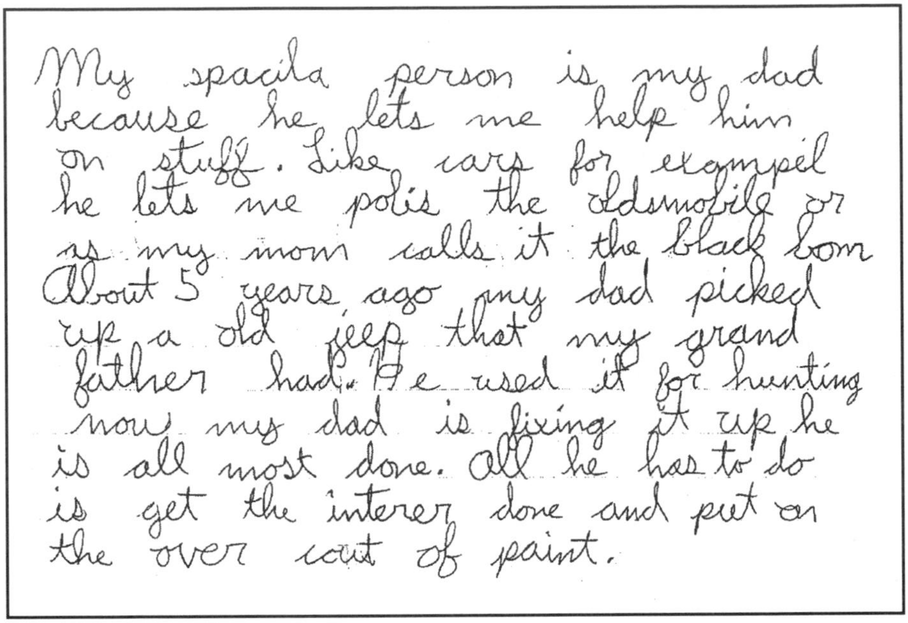

My spacila person is my dad because he lets me help him on stuff. Like cars for exampel he lets me polis the oldsmobile or as my mom calls it the black bom About 5 years ago my dad picked up a old jeep that my grand father had. He used it for hunting now my dad is fixing it up he is all most done. All he has to do is get the interer done and put on the over caut of paint.

Figure 5.1 Joe's "special person" piece

- Because the brand name of the car (*Oldsmobile*) was important to him, he paid attention to its correct spelling.
- Although he was unable to self-correct them from first to second draft, he identified five of the seven words that were misspelled in the piece—an important first step toward editing proficiency.

If the research group hadn't made a commitment to work from students' strengths in analyzing their spelling, we might have been discouraged by a piece like Joe's, which, while full of voice and well-chosen details, contains a disproportionate amount of errors for its length. By focusing our product analysis on what he could do (or could almost do) rather than on what he couldn't, we were able to see his work in a different light. This stance allowed us to think through appropriate teaching points: in Joe's case, a mini-lesson about how to arrive at correct spelling for words he identified as potential problems.

We also learned that product analysis could help students evaluate their own progress in spelling over the course of the year. In late May, Judy asked each of her second graders to edit a journal entry he or she had written during September. After students had done the best they could with their pieces, the class gathered on the rug to debrief the experience. According to

Judy, "There were a lot of comments about how they wrote at the beginning of the year. Kids said things like, 'Look at the way I spelled that! I know how to spell it now.'" Not only did this activity provide concrete evidence of students' growth, but it also offered the opportunity for students to name what they had learned as spellers—an important step in their metacognitive development (Brown, Armbruster, and Baker 1986).

Product analysis also sparked Martha's discovery lesson with a small group of learners whose writing samples suggested confusion about how to spell the /k/ sound at the end of a one-syllable word. "I created a set of thirty cards with words spelled with vowel-*c-k* (e.g., *kick* or *pack*), with vowel-vowel-*k* (e.g., *peek* or *hook*), and vowel-*k-e* (e.g., *snake* or *choke*)," she wrote. She continued:

> I selected my first group—Dory, Alexia, Josh, and Sarah—because each of them was good at explaining their thinking and already had a good eye for spelling. I started by explaining what I had noticed in their writing and that I thought they were ready to discover what the rule would be for spelling the sound of /k/. I told them all the words had /k/ at the end of the word and asked them to sort the cards by pattern.
>
> They began sorting the cards into two piles, one with -*ck* and the other with -*k* and -*ke*. They were calling the latter pile the "just *K*" words, so I asked them to take another look at the "just *K*" pile. Could they sort them even more? Well, yes, they could, and they created a third pile that separated the vowel-*k-e* words from the vowel-vowel-*k* words.
>
> They thought they were done, but I surprised them when I asked them to talk until they discovered the rule that governed when to use -*ck* or -*k*. I guided their thinking by asking them to read the lists aloud. That still wasn't triggering any response, so I asked them to sound just the vowel part of the word. As they read the lists, Alexia was first to articulate that the words with short vowels were spelled with -*ck* and the ones with long vowels were spelled with -*k* or vowel-*k-e*. "Oh, oh, oh," she exclaimed. "What are you thinking?" I asked. "I think that these ones are, um, uh, -*ck*," she began. "The vowels are—I forgot what they're called, but they go, 'Ahhh,' 'Ihhh,' and these ones, " she said, pointing to another pile, "go 'Ayyy.'"
>
> These are "the rules" my students came up with:
> - If it's just a -*k*, there's always two vowels in the word, like in *creek*, *peek*, and *croak*.
> - If it's just -*k-e*, there's always a vowel on the other side [of the *k*].
> - If it's -*ck*, there's always a [short] vowel before it.

This lesson was effective because the students Martha selected were those who were just on the edge of discovering these generalizations for themselves. Without a thoughtful analysis of their writing she could not have determined their readiness.

Our research-group talk also helped us think in more complex ways about spelling tests as a kind of product that could be analyzed. When Enola began teaching second grade a year ago, she returned to the comfort of an old spelling series that was still floating around school. Although she wasn't entirely comfortable with this approach, she could live with it while she adjusted to a new grade level. It wasn't too long, however, before Frank, one of her students, raised the inevitable question: "Why do we have to have spelling tests?"

"Funny you should ask that," Enola answered, "because I have been asking myself the same question. I'm not sure that spelling tests are the best way to learn how to spell. How else do you think we learn?"

Over the next few weeks, the students consulted their parents on this subject, developed a list of other spelling strategies, and talked about ways they could individualize their spelling lists if they did decide to be tested. Eventually, they voted on whether to take tests at all, with only four children—all girls—deciding they would. Over the course of the year, however, all but two of the sixteen kids opted to begin taking spelling tests again. Their reasons varied: Some of them felt they learned better that way, some of them were clearly getting reinforcement about the value of tests from home, and others seemed to like the predictable routine of a new list at the beginning of each week followed by a test at the end.

During our inquiry, we consulted a variety of resources on spelling tests, and most authors had reservations about the potential of tests to foster lasting growth in spelling. Like Enola's second graders, however, a few of us decided that we did not necessarily want to give up this tool for assessing and evaluating students' growth as spellers. Consequently, with help from Wilde (1997), we developed the list of criteria for testing in our building that appears in the Tip on the next page.

In the research group, we also experimented with the index of control (Laminack and Wood 1996) as an alternative to testing. This procedure permitted us to compare the number of words spelled conventionally in a given piece of writing to the number of different words used in the piece (see the Tip "Determining an Index of Control" on p. 114 for a step-by-step summary of how to do this). When a student's total number of different words in a piece increased and the index of control remained consistent or

T I P

Criteria for Spelling Tests

- Use a small number of words: no more than three per week for primary-age children, no more than six for fourth or fifth graders. Using too many words makes it too difficult for us to monitor them and hold students accountable for learning them.
- Use personalized lists. Too many equity issues are raised by a standard list: Some children are always working over their heads, while others are never challenged.
- Provide regular time for children to practice with a room buddy who has similar spelling needs. This ensures that students' opportunities to learn do not depend upon their having strong academic support at home. Although many of our children do, some do not.
- Have children practice with the "look, say, cover, write, check" method, not with commercial worksheets.
- Set expectations for transfer into students' writing. Every so often, we ask students to go through their work and make sure the words they've learned are spelled correctly.
- Use multiple methods of collecting data about students as spellers. Those of us who do still employ tests no longer rely on them as the sole source of information about students' spelling.

improved, we had a piece of evidence to support spelling growth. When the index of control rose but the number of different words in the piece did not, we needed to consider the possibility that the student might have "shifted the emphasis from expression of ideas and word choice" to using words he or she was confident about spelling (Laminack and Wood 1996, 50). For this reason, the index of control helped us gauge students' risk taking as well as their control of convention in a way that a simple percentage of correct spelling could not.

Although this method was a little awkward for most of us to use at first, it offered us a way to generate numerical data about students' spelling that could be tracked over time and examined for patterns. Unlike a number of other evaluation strategies, the index of control was applicable to students' work as it naturally occurred, and therefore it did not require us to give up valuable class time to gather data in a decontextualized situation. And, as Martha pointed out, doing the calculations on pieces of writing was a way for parent volunteers to help out with spelling that didn't involve correcting and tallying tests.

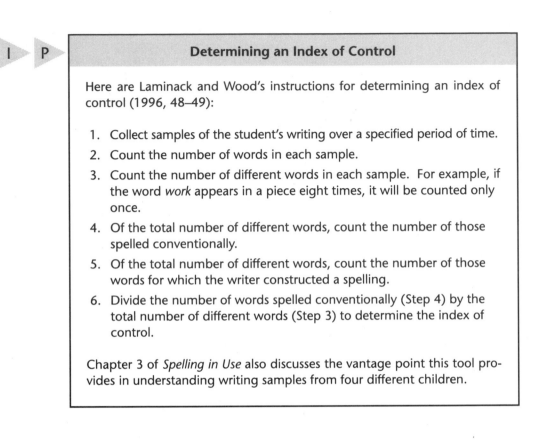

T I P

Determining an Index of Control

Here are Laminack and Wood's instructions for determining an index of control (1996, 48–49):

1. Collect samples of the student's writing over a specified period of time.
2. Count the number of words in each sample.
3. Count the number of different words in each sample. For example, if the word *work* appears in a piece eight times, it will be counted only once.
4. Of the total number of different words, count the number of those spelled conventionally.
5. Of the total number of different words, count the number of those words for which the writer constructed a spelling.
6. Divide the number of words spelled conventionally (Step 4) by the total number of different words (Step 3) to determine the index of control.

Chapter 3 of *Spelling in Use* also discusses the vantage point this tool provides in understanding writing samples from four different children.

One of the pivotal learnings of our inquiry project, however, was the rich source of data that products beyond individually authored pieces of writing could be. As the Interludes in this book demonstrate, many of us used whole-class charts and brainstorming lists as another window on what students knew and could articulate about spelling. Previous to our research, we certainly used these techniques in our teaching, but we did not mine them for insights and patterns as we have since learned to do.

Developing a Schoolwide Rubric

Two factors led us to develop a schoolwide rubric for spelling. First, our research had pushed us to a place where we could no longer live with the discrepancy between our new knowledge and our old evaluation system. The more data we gathered about students' spelling from observations, conferencing, and product analysis, the more uncomfortable we felt about reducing students' learning to a single letter on the report card. At the same time, we received a clear message from our students' parents that they wanted spelling to be graded separately (see Chapter 4). Rather than trying to lobby for change in our district while simultaneously trying to change the parents' minds, we decided to devise a reporting tool that would better communicate the complexity of students' learning to parents and other stakeholders as well as help us avoid conflict with colleagues from other schools.

So, on the final day of our summer retreat, having spent an entire week talking and writing about spelling, we began to draft a rubric for spelling evaluation that could be used schoolwide to supplement the report card. For us, writing the rubric was a three-step process, with lots of conversation and chart-paper scrawlings at each stage.

Reminded by Rief and Barbieri (1994) that what we value should be at the heart of evaluation, we asked ourselves two questions: "What do we value about spellers?" and "What do good spellers do?" Then we brainstormed the following list:

Good Spellers
- self-correct
- use a variety of strategies effectively/appropriately
- spell frequently used words correctly
- take risks
- make attempts at unknown words
- make close approximations
- identify words that are spelled incorrectly
- understand when correct spelling is important
- use spelling resources appropriately
- show developmental growth toward conventional spelling

After we had a list that was connected to our overall hopes for student spellers, we moved to the next level of scrutiny: deciding which elements were most appropriate for this particular tool. This discussion led us to exclude a few items we had brainstormed. For example, we eliminated the item on risk taking because we decided it was too subjective and too difficult to document. We also felt that this attitude was related by behaviors described by the rubric that were easier to pinpoint, such as "makes attempts at unknown words."

We also talked about how to sequence the descriptors. In our initial draft, the bullet about strategic behaviors appeared before the one about degree of correctness. Later, we reversed the order because we wanted to emphasize, even with the organization of our evaluation tool, that correctness was indeed our ultimate goal. While we certainly wanted students to exhibit the other behaviors listed in the rubric, there wasn't much use in them if they didn't eventually lead to an improvement in students' ability to spell conventionally.

After we decided on the elements we wanted to include and established their order, the final step was to write descriptors at the "A," "B," "C," and "D" level for each of them (see Figure 5.2 for the document we finally

Figure 5.2 Schoolwide rubric for spelling

Mapleton Elementary School
Evaluation Criteria for Spelling

An "A" speller:
- spells all or nearly all words correctly in writing
- identifies and self-corrects misspelled words all or nearly all the time
- attempts to spell all or nearly all unknown words
- uses a variety of spelling strategies and resources efficiently
- adjusts expectations for correctness sensitively depending upon purpose for writing

A "B" speller:
- spells most words correctly in writing
- identifies and self-corrects misspelled words most of the time
- attempts to spell most unknown words
- uses a variety of spelling strategies and resources
- adjusts expectations for correctness effectively depending upon purpose of writing

A "C" speller:
- spells some words correctly in writing
- identifies and self-corrects misspelled words some of the time
- attempts to spell some unknown words
- uses a few spelling strategies and resources
- makes some adjustments in expectations for correctness depending upon purpose of writing

A "D" speller:
- spells few words correctly in writing
- seldom identifies and self-corrects misspelled words
- attempts to spell few unknown words
- uses one or no spelling strategies or resources
- makes no adjustments for correctness depending upon purpose of writing

agreed upon). According to our rubric, for example, a student who efficiently used a variety of spelling strategies (e.g., using known words, breaking the word into syllables, using the dictionary) would be working at the "A" level, while a child who relied on only a couple of strategies exclusively (e.g., sounding out and asking for help) would be working at the "C" level. During this stage of the process, we were mostly concerned with making each descriptor parallel with those in other letter-grade categories and writing the standards clearly enough that we could use them to distinguish among different levels of performance. Everyone received a draft of the rubric after it had been edited. We resolved to use it in the fall and see whether we needed to make changes.

Field-Testing the Rubric

One of our concerns as we wrote the rubric was that students might not be able to understand the language of the document—that it would be a tool teachers would need to "translate" for use in the classroom on a daily basis. While this is undoubtedly true for those of us who work in the primary grades ("self-correction" is probably not a familiar term for most of Lois and Lynne's six-year-olds), we discovered when Gail introduced the rubric to her fifth graders that older students were perfectly capable of making sense of the descriptors. In fact, some of them might have been able to write them just as easily as we did.

Gail began the conversation about the rubric by asking the students to address the same question we had tackled during our retreat: "What do good spellers do?" Here's a sampling from the list they generated:

> "They practice words they don't know. They write them down and practice them." (Terence)
> "If they don't know how to spell something, they try a bunch of different strategies." (Jan)
> "They check their writing after they write." (Myles)
> "They think about rules they know: like *i* before *e*, unless it has that *-gh* thing." (Jay)

Next, Gail put a copy of the rubric on the overhead. As she uncovered the descriptors one by one, she asked students to put them in their own words. "Tell me what you think that means," she said, showing them the bullet that read "identifies and self-corrects misspelled words all or nearly all the time." In response to her questions, "What would that look like on your paper? How would I know you could do that?" the students had the following answers:

JENNA: There'd be a lot of circled words.
JUSTIN: And erase marks.
TERENCE: No, you shouldn't erase. There'd be lots of words off to the side.
JUSTIN: Or words above it.
MS. GIBSON: I'm curious about this erasing thing. Why wouldn't you want to erase?
DEVON: 'Cause you want to know our mistakes, so you can work with us on them.

When Gail moved on to the next descriptor, "attempts to spell all or nearly all unknown words," students were just as confident:

MYLES: You wouldn't just go ask the teacher.
JAY: You'd try to learn hard words you didn't know.
ILSA: We don't just say, "I can't spell that word." You try it on your own.

Other highlights of the conversation included Jan's definition of a strategy ("a bunch of different ways you can use to help you figure out things") and the thirteen-item list of spelling resources the students generated.

The only descriptor on the rubric that gave the fifth graders pause was the last one: "adjusts expectations for correctness sensitively depending upon purpose for writing." "How would I know you were able to do that?" Gail asked. Then she offered an example to help them when they looked at her with blank faces: "If you were writing a letter to the superintendent of schools and you were writing notes to yourself in social studies class, would your expectations for spelling be the same?" After a few seconds and an unfinished thought from Devon, Terence said, "Oh, yeah. It's like when the teacher's talking and you have to quickly copy down what they're saying and keep going. Some words might not be spelled correctly. But when you're writing a letter, they should all be spelled right."

"In your notes you're writing a lot of abbreviations, and you're trying to keep it really short," Justin added. "If you're writing a letter, you're trying to make it long and have everything spelled out right."

The video of this conversation was affirming to research-group members in several ways. It demonstrated that students could indeed engage with the language of the rubric and that their understanding of good spelling was consistent with ours. Although some fine-tuning of the rubric was probably going to be necessary as we used it over time, the basic principles behind it were sound. The video also showed that our work in the previous year had affected the way students approached spelling. According to Gail, "It showed how much instruction they had gotten from Kim and Lorna. I've been teaching for twenty-five years—in the past, my students could not have articulated the kind of knowledge about spelling until the end of the year that these students were discussing in the first month of fifth grade."

We cannot tell you much more about the rubric's success (or lack of it), since we are using it for the first time to evaluate students' progress as this book goes to press. What we can share is how optimistic we are about its potential to establish a common set of standards for spelling across the school. "It should establish a consistent program for students as they progress through the grades," Martha writes. She adds:

> Even though students will have teachers with different teaching styles, those teachers will have common goals. The process we went through to write the rubric helped us define those habits we value in spellers. It will also give us a guide to inform our teaching since we cannot rate students against a scale if we don't teach what is on that scale.

Lyn Edgecomb, a fifth-grade teacher who joined our staff after we developed the rubric, had the following to say about it:

> I am hoping for more uniformity: a "B" speller in fourth grade will be a "B" speller in fifth, or perhaps improve to an "A" speller, but there won't be as many chances for a child to get "A"s in fourth (for whatever reason—good tests, low grades in every other area and the one place to boost his ego) and then become a "C" speller in fifth because he really cannot perform outside the study/test situation, etc. It also gives me a more valid tool for evaluation, meaning I can now more easily justify to parents why their child is getting a particular grade in spelling when the parents come in and say, "You didn't give any tests, how can you give a grade in spelling?"

We will need to collect data about our use of the rubric and responses to it by students and parents. In a sense, we will all be working on this research question: "What happens when a group of teachers implements a commonly developed evaluation tool?" We don't know the answers to this question yet, but we're certainly interested in finding out!

So-Far Reflections and Hopes for the Future

Our inquiry helped us learn to evaluate students' spelling more effectively on a daily basis and to use that information to provide more sensitive instruction. Just as important, we finally managed to design a summative evaluation tool that was aligned with our day-to-day, formative evaluation and therefore helped to tie curriculum, instruction, and assessment together in a more coherent fashion.

Ultimately, we realized that whether or not we are able to use the rubric we developed hinges on our ability to evaluate data from the three sources—observations, conferencing, and product analysis—discussed here. By themselves, none of these tools can provide us with information about students' performance on each of the five indicators of the rubric. Product analysis without observation will not tell us whether students are able to use spelling strategies and resources; observation without conferencing will not indicate whether students adjust their expectations for spelling depending upon a writing task. These categories are interdependent, and each of them can provide a basis for the judgments about individual students' progress that we will record on a rubric every nine weeks. The information we report to parents will be anchored in data and grounded in a shared understanding—by both teachers and students—of what it means to be a proficient speller.

We hope to make our spelling assessment and evaluation so seamless with the rest of our teaching that we'll have no further need for the EZ Grader. We'll need no more elaborate schemes to reconcile our student-centered philosophy with test-centered evaluation. This will undoubtedly be a long process—one we've only just begun—but we're confident that collaborative classroom-based inquiry will help us reach our destination. Perhaps the following Extensions will encourage you to make the same trip.

Extensions

1. Make a list of the characteristics you associate with good spellers. Then ask your students—as individuals, as a group, or both—to make a simi-

lar list. Compare your lists and see whether the same things are mentioned. If the documents are similar, rejoice! If they're not, think about how you can close the gap between your conceptions (for example, through a carefully planned series of mini-lessons).

2. Choose one student whom you know fairly well, and freewrite a paragraph about him or her as a speller using our rubric descriptors (or your own criteria) as a starting point. Writing a paragraph from memory will probably help allay any fears you may have (fears initially shared by several members of our research group) that you won't be able to "keep track" of all the information included in the rubric. (We think you will.)

3. Just in case you don't have all that data stored in your head for all students, you may want to devise a one-page form with all of your students' names on it, and use it periodically during writing time to keep anecdotal records about spelling behavior you observe.

INTERLUDE

"I Know *You* Have": Students Talk About Their Spelling Improvement

GAIL GIBSON, GRADE 5

I always spend a lot of time during the first weeks of school assessing my students' knowledge and understanding about literacy. Since becoming involved with teacher research, I've discovered that one of the most effective methods is simply asking the students to tell me what they know while I take notes. Scripting the conversation allows me to look for patterns and to reflect more deeply at a later time on what the students said. It also allows me to share the students' comments and get feedback from other staff members.

In this session, with Kelly's help, I selected three students who were representative of the range of spellers in my class. I knew from their participation in classroom discussions that they would be able to articulate their ideas about spelling. I gave the students the questions about fifteen minutes before the actual discussion. (Those questions are indicated in the following dialogues by boldface type.) I asked them to think about their answers but not to discuss them amongst themselves until the interview. They could (and did) take notes on their papers before the discussion.

We met in my office next to the computer. I asked the students if they would like me to input their answers on the computer. Their reply was, "You type and we'll talk." And talk they did!

Ms. Gibson: **Has your spelling improved since the beginning of last year, and if so, how?**

Ilsa: Having the spelling meeting last year helped because talking about a word you don't know how to spell helps my spelling. If you talk more about the word, it makes you remember it more.

Ms. Gibson: What did you talk about?

Ilsa: You talk about where you found the word. The teacher asked where you found it and what it meant. And then she asked how you spelled it right.

Devon: You have to know how to say the word, not just spell it.

Terence: The more you talk about it the more you remember it.

Ms. Gibson: Are you better spellers than you were then?

All three: Yes!

Terence [*stopping to think about the question some more*]: Weelll, sort of . . .

Ilsa: I'm not a very good speller, but I'm better than I used to be. I know what to do to spell it right, but I still get some words wrong.

Devon: I think I am [a better speller].

Terence [*turning to face Devon and patting him on the head*]: I *know* you are.

Ilsa: Last year we worked on two strategies a week. The teacher would give us a word, and we could only use that strategy to spell the word she gave us. Then we could use that strategy throughout the week . . . like breaking the word into smaller parts. That one helped me a lot.

Devon: Sounding it out.

Terence: Like the worksheet we did last week.

The worksheet was based on the word *sincerely*. I had noticed in the thank-you notes the students wrote earlier that many of them were misspelling it. The letters on the sheet were scrambled, and the task was to write as many two-letter words, three-letter words, and so on, as they could, then finally to unscramble the "big word." They were also to underline any of the words that could be found in *sincerely* (e.g., *in, sin, rely*). I hoped this would help them remember the correct spelling. More important, I wanted to reinforce the strategy of looking for little words they already knew inside big words they needed to get right.

TERENCE: Sometimes when you're writing you have the letters right, but they are in the wrong place, like the word *school,* and you need to unscramble them. That reminded me of spelling little words inside big words so you get them right.

ILSA: At the beginning of last year, say I wrote a letter—I would read through the letter and I would find about two words that were spelled wrong. This year if I write a letter, I usually find all the words [that are spelled wrong].

MS. GIBSON: How does that show you are a better speller?

ILSA: I can tell when they are spelled wrong easily now.

TERENCE [*to Ilsa*]: Just like in *Maniac Magee*—you have to prove it.

Terence was commenting on my follow-up question to Ilsa and connecting it to the classroom, where we were reading *Maniac Magee* (Spinelli 1990) together. Just that day we had read the section where Maniac, the main character, tries to teach his friend Grayson to read. The students really enjoyed Spinelli's explanation of how difficult vowels are to understand in comparison to consonants. I had asked the students to prove his theory was right, just as I had asked Ilsa to back up her statement.

DEVON: This year when we were doing that test with Mrs. Morrison and we looked at the words list—when the words got longer, you have to pay more attention. I'm better at longer words now.

TERENCE: Last year, most words I didn't know how to spell. Like Devon said, when Mrs. Morrison tested us, I can spell longer words. I know to check other places to see if the words are spelled right, too. If you read the word in enough books, it makes it easier to spell because you've looked at it so many times.

Once again, Terence was relating his understandings about spelling to classroom experiences. Vicky Morrison, an educational technician and a member of the research group, had been helping me gather data about individual students by administering several word inventories.

ILSA: It reminded me of how at my church when we do plays, you have to look at the script so many times it's stuck in your head. It's just like spelling . . . the words are stuck in our head.

TERENCE: It's like music in chorus, too. The words are stuck in our head because we sing them so many times.

Ms. GIBSON: **How do you students help each other with spelling in your classroom?**

DEVON: I helped Justin spell *million*, then he could spell *billion*. He had *million* stuck in his head more. We don't use *billion* as much as *million* in math.

TERENCE: Most people have millions of dollars instead of billions. The main idea is we use million a lot more. When you are helping somebody, it's best not to tell them. You could say, "What word do you hear at the end of *send?*" and then they'd get it right after a while. You know, little words or part of words. That helped me a lot.

ILSA: With my little brother, just for fun, he likes me to say words and he tries to spell them. I gave him a word and he had no clue how to spell it. It had a smaller word in it, and I said, "How do you spell that?" and he got it right. Then I said "What would come before it?" and "What would come after it?" and he got the whole word. At night in bed—we share a room—he wants me to ask him words to spell. He thinks it's fun.

TERENCE: I don't think they should look in a dictionary. How are they ever going to learn how to spell it if all they do is look in the dictionary? You just look it up and that's it.

ILSA AND DEVON: How can you look it up if you can't spell it?

TERENCE: Just give them the first three letters. If they know what the word looks like, but they don't know how to spell it, then they can find it.

ILSA: If you can't find it and the teacher tells you how to spell it and then you have to look it up anyway . . . What's the point of that?

TERENCE: If you know the first three letters and you know the ending sound you can spell it.

DEVON: Like *new* and *knew*.

TERENCE: No, like *s-t-a-* and then you know the last letter. You can find the word because of the way it looks. Words look different.

ILSA: How can you look it up if you can't spell it?

TERENCE: Yes, you can, if you have three letters. Where is the dictionary in here, and I'll show you how it works. You can know what the word looks like and not know how to spell it.

DEVON: What do you mean?

Ms. GIBSON: Do you mean the shape—short and tall letters?

TERENCE: No two words are spelled the same anyway. Of course you can find it.

ILSA: Yes, they are.

An argument erupted here, with Devon and Ilsa saying it wasn't true— words can be spelled the same—and Terence arguing that they are all different. I wrote the word *bank* twice. Terence immediately gave two definitions and said, "Oh, you had to be right. You proved me wrong. Why don't they just call one a slope?"

Ms. Gibson: **What do you think the readers of our book, other teachers, should know about teaching spelling to kids?**

Ilsa: Be nice about it. Don't say, "Look it up in the dictionary" when you've been looking for a long time. Not that any teacher in this building would ever say that.

Terence: Sometimes words are hard, and we need help . . . a clue.

Devon: Last year Kelly wouldn't tell me how to spell a word. Then I asked her if she would help me. She told me to write down all the words I knew. I can show you 'cause I still have it in my notebook at home. I told her all the words I could spell and put them together and then I got it. And I've still got it and that's how I spell words all the time now. It works.

Terence: Like *c* or *k* words. We need some help. If I knew how it spell it, why would I be here asking? Give them some ideas they can use—different ways. You don't want to waste time or get discouraged, and you want to remember the word, too. You really want to write your ideas down, not waste time looking in the dictionary.

The dismissal bell rang just as Terence finished his final words of advice. We ended the conversation and began to get ready to go home. But Ilsa couldn't resist one final comment . . .

Ilsa [*whispered to herself*]: I still don't think looking it up in the dictionary makes sense.

After the students left, I returned to the computer and reread the script of our discussion. It clearly showed that the students knew a lot about spelling. It showed they were able to articulate and evaluate effective strategies. It showed they were able to relate their understanding of spelling to other classroom activities. However, the script did not reveal the enthusiasm with which they approached the interview, nor their smiles and nods as they complimented each other and validated each other's comments. Most important, it did not show the hours of planning and instruction that had occurred in their fourth-grade classrooms, nor the support that both fourth-grade teachers received from other members of the research group. If I had a strong foundation to build on with these spellers (and their comments certainly suggested I did), then I had more than one person to thank.

Pulling Together: Beginning and Sustaining an Inquiry Group on Spelling

When we were on our teacher-research retreat last summer, the biggest thunderstorm any of us had ever seen swept over Millinocket Lake. The wind whipped up huge swells, creating whitecaps that looked more like the ocean than fresh water. Since we were safe in the lodge with the windows shut, none of us was very concerned. Then we realized that our host's float-plane was in jeopardy of being dashed against the dock, and Lynne and Diane joined the camp staff who were working to hold it steady. For twenty minutes or so, until the storm passed, they stood gripping one of the plane's wings and pushing it away from both the dock and the shore.

That night at dinner, Diane told us about being a part of the plane's "crew." She joked about how initially she and Lynne had been doing exactly the wrong thing in their desire to help the cause. Until their efforts were directed and coordinated by the camp staff, who had experienced such storms before, they weren't doing much good. "But once we got pulling in the right direction," Diane related with a wry grin, "it really made a difference." After the laughter subsided, Vicky said thoughtfully, "Isn't that the way it is with everything?"

That's definitely the way it was with our research group. Our work on spelling was far more powerful because we were all "pulling" in the same direction. Our collaborative inquiry was further enriched by the participation of students, parents, and the "distant teachers" (John-Steiner 1985) whose writing we read. By drawing on them and each other, we were finally able to make tangible progress toward resolving our tensions about spelling and developing consistent, effective instruction for our students.

We hope that the previous chapters piqued your curiosity about our inquiry process or, better yet, sparked your interest in pursuing collaborative inquiry yourself. Our intention with this final chapter is to provide enough detail about how our particular inquiry group works so that you can begin thinking about what *you* might need to support your own classroom-based research about spelling (or, for that matter, any other topic you identify as important to your teaching). We've identified a series of conditions that, from our experience, need to be in place for inquiry groups to pull together and be successful. Each is discussed below.

Pulling Together Requires a Common Direction

We see spelling inquiry as one of the easiest ways for teachers to begin teacher research. As Lois explains,

> Spelling is a really concrete topic. It's easy to collect student samples and other kinds of data without getting bogged down with too many observational notes. It's also a topic that parents and the general public are highly concerned about, so it's good to be able to say, "We're looking at this. We want to know what kids do, what we should be doing, and what parents can do." People are interested (as was evident in our parent surveys) and curious.

We're familiar with some thriving school-based inquiry groups where members come together to discuss a wide range of inquiry projects (see Meyer, Larson, and Zetterman 1998 and Allen, Cary, and Delgado 1995 for examples). What unites these groups is their common interest in improving their practice through inquiry and reflection, not a particular topic or instructional objective. Depending upon your particular school context, this model may work better for you than ours. (See Figure 6.1 for a summary of the benefits of both models.)

For us, however, an "umbrella topic" (Harvey 1998) such as spelling provides cohesiveness and a sense of common purpose. Our questions are richer and more complex because everyone has had a hand in shaping them. It's easier to trust our conclusions because we have a natural way to cross-check them with each other.

Advantages of Individually Chosen Topics for Inquiry	Advantages of Umbrella Topics for Inquiry
• Motivation and investment are increased when teachers, like student writers (see Graves 1983), choose their topics. • Teachers can address immediate issues in their classrooms with their work. • Majority rule does not leave members feeling disgruntled if their topic suggestions were not adopted by the group. • The diversity of different topics enriches everyone; members learn from each other's work.	• Isolation is reduced; teachers have a common sense of purpose. • There is room for different levels of commitment among members. • The work of a group often has more credibility with others than the work of an individual teacher does. • The work of the group can be more easily connected to reform efforts in curriculum and assessment.

Figure 6.1 Models for inquiry

Regardless of whether you start with an umbrella topic or an unfettered choice, we think collaboration with others is key. We don't mean to discourage you from beginning an inquiry project if you work in a school setting where it will be difficult to enlist research partners. Nor do we mean to suggest that the efforts of individual teacher researchers are less significant than the work of groups. But we do see unique benefits to working within a collaborative structure, and we agree with Dorothy Strickland that while teacher research "may be the ultimate in professional development," it "really requires a supportive community . . . It's just too hard to do it all by yourself" (quoted in Glazer 1998, 168).

A number of us who have chosen to be part of the research group would probably not pursue inquiry individually. It takes an incredible amount of time and energy to be a solo teacher researcher, just as it does to power a single scull on a river. By rowing a boat with multiple oarlocks, so to speak, we draw motivation from one another. We're also able to rest sometimes—to take a break from the oar when other commitments intrude—because fellow group members are willing to pull harder at a particular time.

Pulling Together Requires Regular Communication

For us, monthly meetings are the glue that holds our common inquiry together. Group members' schedules and the vagaries of the school calendar don't allow us to schedule them on the same day of the week consistently, although many of them do fall on Tuesdays, the day set aside for biweekly faculty meetings. When Gail is able to condense the staff-meeting agenda, we're able to include research-group talk time in these contractually required sessions—which means that more people are able to participate. Otherwise, attendance is an above-and-beyond-the-call-of-duty commitment that we make because, in Judy's words, "being part of a caring, supportive research group has been a wonderful learning experience and well worth the extra time it requires."

Our gatherings begin in the teachers' room both because it's the most comfortable place in the school, with couches and easy access to the coffee maker, and because it's a central location, where passersby might get drawn into our conversation and stay a while. Official meetings are scheduled for ninety minutes, from 3:00 to 4:30, but our talk often continues during dinner at a local restaurant for people who can spare the time. (Martha has even developed the habit of leaving chop suey for her husband to heat up so she'll be free to go out on research-group nights.)

We've found that we do some of our best thinking and writing in these nonschool settings. After drafting our first grant proposal on a Ruby Tuesday's napkin and our second-year budget on a Chinese-restaurant placemat, we've learned to take a notebook and a pen to these evening meals. In addition, our grant allows us to schedule occasional sessions for specific purposes: a planning meeting for our spelling conference, a Saturday-morning writing session for this book, a weekend retreat in January to do midyear data analysis.

A typical research-group meeting may include a variety of activities (see the Tip on the next page, "Ways to Use Inquiry Group Time," for a list of possibilities). The following elements are consistent, however:

- We begin with an agenda that Kelly draws up in consultation with other members of the research group. Although we're willing to add or delete items if the group needs to go in a different direction, we've found that a plan helps us stay focused.
- We document what we accomplish by keeping minutes stored on a laptop computer and saving any charts or lists we make.

T ▶ I ▶ P

Ways to Use Inquiry Group Time

1. Begin with a five-to-ten-minute freewrite on a topic or a question (e.g., "What have you learned from your inquiry project so far?"). Then ask members to share excerpts or to summarize what they wrote about.

2. Discuss a selected reading that everyone has read, and/or set aside time for members to report on their individual reading. (See Appendix A for our recommendations on spelling and teacher research.)

3. Ask everyone to bring a piece of data from her classroom (a sample of student writing, an entry from her anecdotal records) and share them around the circle. During one of our early meetings, for example, members came prepared to discuss or demonstrate an example of students' strategy use as spellers.

4. Have a round-robin oral share around a prompt, such as "Talk about something interesting you've noticed in your classroom since we last met."

5. Analyze a set of data from one member's classroom. In the past, our group has done the following:
   - coded students' responses to a few questions Lorna asked her fourth graders about their literature discussion groups
   - identified spelling patterns in science writing for Martha's four case-study students
   - sorted and classified Post-its with items from Lois's teaching journal that pertained to her research question on the effects of teacher read-alouds on first graders' reading, writing, and speaking
   - compared the different ways Kim's fourth graders chose to spell each syllable of *quadricep*

6. Brainstorm and refine research plans together (see Chapter 2 for details).

- We devote a considerable amount of time to informal talk and try to ensure that everyone's voice is heard during a session.
- We ground this talk in specific data from our classrooms.

The last item on this list represents an important way that we prevent our conversations from being infected by negativity and complaints. In the past, when our discussions were general, it was easy to focus on immediate concerns and lose sight of more long-term goals. In contrast, discussions that start with student work or observations help us consider both the here-and-now ("What does this child know about spelling?") and the long view ("What do we want her work to look like when she leaves here, and how do we help her get there?"). This is not to say that we're Pollyannas or that we're pleased with every piece of student work we examine—far from it. But we're more able to be balanced and analytical in our approach when we begin with that kind of data.

Related to these ideas is our general avoidance of the term "support group" to describe our work since, for many people, this phrase connotes a temporary way to cope with weakness or adversity. While teaching is certainly a challenging job (for which we welcome all the support we can get), the benefits we gain from our meetings are more than a pat on the back or an understanding ear—although these are certainly important aspects of our time together. We're asking important questions about teaching and learning, and we don't expect to find easy answers and then discontinue our membership. For these reasons, we usually speak of the "research group" or "inquiry group"—phrases that emphasize both the importance of our questions and the systematic nature of our collaboration.

Although our monthly meetings are the centerpiece of our work together, our research-group message board is another way we create space for talk about our inquiry. This message board is a pad of chart paper standing permanently on an easel in our teachers' room. When Kelly borrowed the easel from Gail's classroom to document our brainstorming during our first meeting, she forgot to take it back that afternoon. She decided not to return it (prompting Gail to order a new easel) after noticing that a number of teachers and staff members who hadn't been at the meeting were reading the chart as they wandered through the teachers' room the next day. At our next session, everyone in the group was invited to use that space to communicate with each other. Here are some of the ways we've used it:

- announcing or reminding members about meeting times and agendas
- posting quotations about teacher research and teaching in general
- posting e-mail messages from Kelly when she is away from Mapleton
- polling everyone on issues of interest (e.g., where to meet, what to read for discussion)
- brainstorming research questions and research designs
- recording notes at our meetings
- posting fliers that might be of interest to the group (e.g., a conference on spelling in Boston)

- posting comic strips, photographs, and poems that relate to our research
- sharing responses from individual members to any of these items and/or to each other's comments

As Martha explained to Kelly in a letter,

> The message board has emerged as an important element [of our research] and emphasizes the importance of recording. This community space allows anyone who stops to have access to our thinking—it must raise questions for those itinerant people who cannot be with us every day. It allows those who haven't bought in officially to remain part of the club. It leaves a trail for you to discover what's been happening while you're away.

> In addition, e-mail has been vital to the group's communication. Since everyone in the school has her own account, reminders and agendas can be sent with a minimum of effort. We also exchange drafts, share data, and offer advice about research questions through electronic messages. If your inquiry group is not based at a single school, e-mail can help you build a strong sense of community. You may even want to set up a listserv (a system where a single e-mail message is sent to all members of a group who have Internet access) so that everyone can keep in touch.

Pulling Together Requires Commitment from Group Members

We won't lie to you—maintaining a successful inquiry group is hard work, and it requires a significant amount of commitment from teachers who are already stretched thin with teaching and family responsibilities. Sometimes we're more committed than others. The good news is that success doesn't have to depend on everyone making the same kinds of contributions at the same time. We hope these profiles of three members—Diane, Jill, and Vicky—will help you see how individual participation may vary.

Diane

During our first year together, Diane attended a couple of early meetings and then decided she didn't need the extra work of being a part of the group. On subsequent meeting days, she went home early or kept a low profile in her kindergarten classroom. "I am a 'do your best or don't bother' kind of person," she writes, "and I knew that teacher research was going to require time, too much time, and too much thought. I was already struggling to find the time necessary for fulfilling my job requirements."

One Tuesday afternoon when the rest of us were gathered, Diane intended to leave school but got distracted by the mess in the lap drawer of her desk. She decided to do some organization before she went home. She notes:

> An hour later, I finished the task, having forgotten about the meeting. Kelly and Gail walked into my room, all excited about the meeting. They wanted to know what I was up to, and the evidence was there: piles of sorted paper clips. Large ones, small ones, colored ones. Was that why I couldn't make the meeting? they asked. I tried to explain it away, but the more I talked, the more absurd it sounded. They tried not to make a big deal out of it, but I was embarrassed and tried to slink out of school.

Later on in the year, Diane found herself at another meeting, almost by accident. "I think someone said to me, 'Oh, you might as well have one of these cinnamon rolls,' as I walked in, and I stayed. I couldn't be quiet." From that point on, "any inkling of interest I showed was accepted," she says. "No one made me feel like they didn't want me to play because I wasn't in on the game from the beginning." For the group, Diane's new perspective was a welcome one. At the same time we were honing our analytical skills—learning to break data into smaller pieces we could code and understand—she reminded us of the importance of seeing that same data holistically. Working from both viewpoints helped us see our inquiry in more complex ways.

Jill

Jill was fighting a life-threatening illness during most of our first year of research, so she joined the group after we had already been together for some time. Her membership was challenging, both mentally and physically, but she persisted:

> Now in remission after having survived cancer, I joined the group a year late. I had such mixed feelings: Could I ever catch up on all the hap-

penings? Where would I fit in? Was I as well-read as everyone else? What could I offer these researchers who were already off to such an enthusiastic beginning?

I nervously attended the first meeting, sitting quietly and trying to absorb it all. I left feeling inadequate and intimidated. I missed the next meeting due to a doctor's appointment, and then at the third one, I sat with butterflies in my stomach, listening to my colleagues discussing their thoughts and ideas with excitement. I wanted so much to feel like I belonged, but I was afraid—afraid of not being able to keep up with the reading and research, afraid that what I'd offer wouldn't be good enough. I left feeling even more confused. Everyone was supposed to pick a research question. *Research* question?! I had too many questions of my own.

I struggled with these feelings for days, finally sharing them with Enola. She made me realize these people would accept me for who I was and where I was coming from. At the next meeting, Kelly reiterated those ideas. She made me understand that not everyone would be at the same starting point and that everyone would be able to go at their own pace. We all have our own experiences and expertise to bring to the group.

Although the other factors in her life made it challenging for Jill to develop a research plan and collect systematic data during the school year, she made a breakthrough as a researcher while participating in our summer retreat. She read several reflections on her spelling instruction during our whole-group sharing time. At the end of the week, she beamed as she said, "I was able to write something I'm proud of. I really feel good about myself." Indeed, one of the pieces she shared was so powerful that, as you have seen, it became the backbone for Chapter 3 of this book.

Vicky

If you are able to establish a research community, there will undoubtedly be people who join it late, although perhaps for different reasons than Diane's or Jill's. Other people may feel uncomfortable about their membership even as they faithfully attend each meeting and work through the group's agenda. Such was the case with Vicky, an educational technician whose interest in observational notetaking led her to join the research group in its first year:

At first I was reluctant, thinking I didn't have anything to offer, but no one pressured me to talk or do anything I didn't want to do. For a long time, I would just go to the meetings and listen (which is usually hard for me to do!). I would go home and all these thoughts would race through my mind. I would write them down in a poem, sometimes sharing them the next day with one or two of the teachers I worked with.

Vicky's role as an ed tech required her to be in multiple classes during the school day. For this reason, some of the group's activities—for example, developing an individual research question—were more awkward for her than others. At the same time, she had a multi-grade perspective that few others in the group had, and she was an experienced notetaker because of her extensive one-on-one work with children. As her poem "Ode to the Researchers" suggests, she needed to figure out how she fit into the group in "her own special way":

Ode to the Researchers

The TV is on; in my head thoughts are welling—
I sit and I think of our meeting on spelling.

Diane and Kim's charts did surely delight;
learning to spell in this way—it seems right.

The children were under no stress to correct;
each spelling itself was a gem to collect.

Should kids choose their words? well, that was the question
on Lorna's mind still, she was now confessing.

With laptop at hand, Kelly tried taking note
of everything said and everyone's quote.

Enola—her kids came up with a list
of ways to spell better, some with a twist,

like using a word off somebody's shirt
Reading plus spelling—they must be alert.

Now Judy ensures that everyone learns—
good spellers with bad, they all take a turn.

And Peggy can find some vowel in their name
to turn spelling into a quite clever game.

Elaine came to see us from the junior high.
Spelling's no different there—I wonder why.

You'd think with these children being much older
They'd take far more risks and be that much bolder.

Spelling with Lois—I'll bet it is fun.
Each child is important, every last one.

Smarty or clueless, no difference at all,
She makes all her students feel ten feet tall.

Where Gail is concerned, I can sure say the same
Working with her is my best claim to fame.

I liked Martha's story of her time with John,
He knew the younger kids couldn't be conned.

So he listened real closely in order to learn
What to tell other students when it was his turn.

It's a sample, you see, that just goes to show:
We all need each other if we're going to grow.

I come to these sessions with not much to say
But I am still learning in my special way.

I feel privileged to have been a part of this group—
It's a good place for me to get the latest scoop.

Last year on reading, and this year on spelling
Sometimes, it's true, it can be overwhelming.

But now that I'm able to listen and learn
someday I'll be ready to take my own turn.

Vicky's participation reminded us of the benefits—both to and from the group—that could be realized when our membership was comprised of more than full-time faculty. For this reason, we began to invite other ed techs, student teachers, and one-on-one aides to our meetings. Although not everyone was able to accept this invitation, some did, and the resulting diversity of perspectives has been healthy for all of us.

Pulling Together Requires a Set of Shared Ground Rules

We feel strongly that our ground rules are one of the reasons it was possible for members as different as Diane, Jill, and Vicky to find their footing in the group. We developed the following list during our first year together, and we have continued to revisit it periodically in order to refresh our memories, renegotiate different elements, and integrate new members:

- Being a part of the group is voluntary. You choose to come, and no one's going to make you feel guilty if you choose not to.
- You get from the group what you need from it. People's participation can take many forms, and that's okay. We are all in different places in our learning, just like our students; the group is flexible enough to accommodate that.
- Your level of participation may ebb and flow over the course of the year. Different people will emerge as leaders as time goes on, depending upon your interests, other time commitments, and family demands.
- The work of the group should make your teaching richer and better. (It should not be just "one more thing" to add to your plate.) If it doesn't, then all of us in the group need to stop and reassess.
- You own your inquiry. Do not feel that you have to choose an area to please someone else or that any question is too small or insignificant.
- The direction of the group and the makeup of meetings should be determined by its members. This is not Kelly's class or Gail's staff-development session. Everyone's voice is equally important, so use yours.

Since these ground rules go against the grain of teacher culture, it has sometimes been hard work to abide by them. When we began our inquiry, many of us shared Diane's "do your best or don't bother" attitude, making it uncomfortable for us to set limits on our participation. If a lively conversation was still going on, it was difficult for people to excuse themselves to pick up their children. If one member had gathered great quantities of data between meetings, other people felt pressured to do the same. A further complication was the resemblance between some of the group's activities (e.g., common readings, freewrites, discussions) and those done in university classes. It was easy to activate our previous schema and assume that everyone needed to do an equal amount of work to get "full credit."

Ultimately, we had to come to grips with the inconsistency between our expectations for ourselves as learners and our expectations for the children in our care. In our classes, we worked hard to acknowledge and celebrate individual differences among our students; we needed to do the same for ourselves. By encouraging people to participate at whatever level was comfortable for them, we were able to increase the diversity of perspectives in the group.

Pulling Together Requires Leadership

In addition to the ground rules, two other factors surfaced as important in helping individuals overcome obstacles to membership: the leadership of the facilitator and that of the principal. Although we believe that personal relationships are the key to strong teacher-research collaborations, we do not think that our group's success can be attributed to the specific personalities of its leaders. The roles that people choose to play in response to the group's needs, not necessarily the people themselves, are what keep the group running smoothly. By discussing these functions here, we hope to help you think about who can play them for you, as well as what roles you might play for others.

The Facilitator

As facilitator, Kelly plays a variety of roles. Because she is based at a university, she has access to more professional resources than the rest of us do, and she can often sift through them and help us decide which would be most worth our limited time. Her flexible schedule allows her to be with us for several days at a time, observing in individual classrooms, gathering data on particular students at members' requests, and covering classes while research partners meet. Other roles for the facilitator that we brainstormed as part of our retreat include:

- modeling for us how to implement strategies or teaching tips
- setting agendas, deadlines, and limits
- keeping track of time during meetings and helping us stay focused
- checking in to see how ideas are evolving, offering support and expertise
- taking our jumbled thoughts and making connections
- linking us with other schools/states/researchers

- helping us find resources (e.g., books, experts, etc.)
- helping us obtain money to do our research

We don't see it as essential to enlist an outside facilitator; teachers within the group can certainly do many of the things listed here. We would, however, recommend designating someone to run meetings who can stay in that job for a while. Rotating this role from month to month doesn't allow anyone to develop the facilitation skills needed to set a "doable" agenda, make sure everyone can be heard, and help people see connections across their ideas.

Another role that Kelly plays is to help group members gather data related to their questions. On a given day, she might interview four students for Gail, do a running record on one child for Judy, and script a whole-class lesson for Martha. Although one of the most commonly cited benefits of having a facilitator was the opportunity to get classroom-based information from another person, several of our group members found this intimidating at first. Apprehension like the kind Lynne expresses here was very common:

> I got excited about having Kelly, our facilitator, come in to my class-room after she visited Lois's room and shared her notes at the lunch table. It was interesting to hear what a quiet observer could notice in one setting. Still, it was a big risk for me to invite her. When she finally did come in, she sat near a cluster of children and began taking notes. There! I didn't have to be nervous. She wasn't watching me; she was interested in the children. Each time she came to visit I became more at ease. She noticed a lot in my classroom that I simply couldn't when I was interacting with the group.

Because most teachers connect observation with evaluation, it's not easy for them to adjust to having another scribbling person in the room—even when they want the data that person can provide. It takes a while for comfortable relationships to evolve. Whether the observer is the group facilitator or a research partner, she or he will need to negotiate participation carefully with the teacher who issued the invitation.

The Principal

Gail plays an unusual role in our group because she splits her time between being principal and teaching language arts to fifth graders. As a longtime teacher-researcher in her classroom, she models the kinds of behavior others in the group are trying to adopt. She has particular credibility with the rest of us because members know she struggles to take notes and keep track of student samples the same way we do.

At the same time, Gail provides support for our inquiry in her role as principal. As Judy explains it, Gail's mentorship puts questions at the forefront of teaching practice:

> She keeps asking us, "Why are you teaching that way? Why do you do what you're doing with your students, and what is your plan?" This has pushed me to reflect, which has improved my teaching and forced me, in a nonthreatening way, to examine myself . . . I don't pretend to know the right way to teach children how to spell, but I am on the road to understanding my students' needs through a clearer appreciation of what they can do and of what next steps they might take toward independence.

In addition to what Judy calls "soft nudges and gentle pushes," Gail's roles in the group include the following:

- ensuring the flexibility to meet curricular goals within our individual classrooms
- encouraging experimentation with new ideas in the classroom
- promoting a community among staff through small presents and surprises
- being a good listener—a sounding board for ideas
- distributing professional reading
- helping members feel comfortable expressing themselves in research-group meetings
- allowing us the freedom to collect research data in our classroom
- being an outside observer and giving feedback in a nonthreatening way
- being diplomatic in many problem situations

If you think that your principal would be interested in classroom-based inquiry, we encourage you to invite him or her to your meetings. Portland, Oregon, principal Kim Campbell (1997a) demonstrates how administrators might take a data-driven, inquiry-based approach to their jobs and therefore be fully participating members of a group. For principals who are more interested in being a part of the conversation than in actively taking part in research, Kim's interview with Deborah Meier, principal of the noted

Central Park East Schools in New York City, discusses some ways that principals can support teacher research in their buildings (Campbell 1997b). Our one note of caution: Be careful that administrators' agendas contribute to but do not supersede the questions that teachers raise for themselves.

The Members

While Kelly and Gail have certain responsibilities in the group, other members take on leadership roles as the need or opportunity arises. If one member's data is the focus of a group discussion, then she generally runs that session. If someone has read a particular resource that no one else is familiar with, then she shares her expertise. During preparation for special events, everyone takes on responsibilities that she can handle. For example, as we were finishing this book (also the same month we were sponsoring a conference), individuals took on a variety of jobs. Lynne was responsible for distributing copies of drafts of this book to everyone for final feedback; Lorna contributed a photo of a student for the cover. Peggy facilitated a planning meeting for the conference; Martha took charge of finishing the brochure to advertise it. These contributions represent more than simple acceptance of already delegated tasks. In each instance, an individual surveyed what needed to be done for the common good, and then determined what she could do to help.

Pulling Together Requires Confidence in Our Potential Contributions

As you've probably guessed from the previous chapters, we see great potential for classroom-based inquiry on spelling to improve instruction in individual classrooms. Conducting their own research can help teachers determine a flexible, data-driven spelling program that is tailored to the needs of a given group of students. And, as Lois reminds us, research on a particular part of your curriculum often has a ripple effect throughout the rest of the day: "Turning the flashlight onto this one area of my teaching has made me much more aware of the rest of it, even when I'm not taking notes or recording. I see more and hear more of the children's comments or their nonparticipation."

Not only did our inquiry help us tune into student data more keenly, but it also led to important conversations about issues related to, but not limited to, spelling. Beginning with a small, narrowly focused topic actually opened up a realm of other possibilities for us, kindling talk about the composition process in general, strategy use, problem solving, and risk taking. Consideration of all of these topics improved our classroom practice.

At the same time that we see its potential for change in individual classrooms, we also believe that teacher research on spelling can—and should—contribute to larger conversations about spelling and literacy in our field. In recent years, there's been an explosion of publications about spelling instruction and a good deal of public concern about the topic. But when we did a literature review on spelling for our grant application, nearly all of the books and articles we encountered had been written by university professors, not full-time classroom teachers. We believe that teachers' voices need to be included in the research literature because teachers are in a unique position to observe strategy use, the role of parents in spelling practice, and the transfer of spelling skills into content areas other than language arts. Who but Kim, the regular classroom teacher, would have been able to capitalize on the opportunity to investigate *quadricep* that arose during gym class? Who but Diane, the regular classroom teacher, would have been able to enhance her understanding of Brent's spelling in kindergarten with information from a conference with his mother, Mrs. Donnelly? If it's true that spelling needs to be understood (and taught) within a broader context of communication, then teachers may be the right people to generate that data. Again, Lois says it best:

> Teachers are the obvious ones to do this research. We're with the workers—the kids—literally "at their elbows" when they are writing and spelling. We get to see what they do and ask "Why did you do that?" No one else sits where we sit, not even parents, really, since I think home is a different environment. Students get used to us because they see us every day, and they get so they can tell us what they are thinking, if we have established a trusting environment.

It took some time before we were ready to embrace the idea that our research could be useful to anyone beyond our immediate context. As we presented our work in local forums—the school board, students in Kelly's methods class, a workshop at a county-level conference—we gained confidence in the importance of our message. We got braver, more willing to give credence to what we had learned from our students and each other. There was a lot of head-nodding and murmurs of agreement among us when Diane said the following during one of our meetings:

> Teacher research forced me to confront my own ideas. Past changes I made in my practice were really compiling other people's thoughts and putting them together, trying to make it work. I was solving problems they had, not my issues. They didn't have a lot to do with what was going on in my room. As long as I could read, I didn't have to think for myself. Now I trust myself, and I'm not just cooking down other people's ideas.

In addition to contributing to conversations about spelling, we hope to contribute to those about classroom-based inquiry. As part of our retreat, everyone completed a freewrite on the following prompt: "What advice do you have for other teachers—individuals and/or members of a group—who want to begin teacher research?" Most of us wrote in general terms about the conditions we saw as crucial for success: time, trust, a willingness to see issues from more than one point of view. Two members of the group approached the task differently, however. Lois chose to address her piece to Jasmine Miller, a close friend who taught at another school and whose "questioning heart" made her a likely candidate to benefit from teacher research:

> Dear Jasmine,
>
> I know that you have a curious mind, a questioning heart, and a will for change. Have you thought about being a teacher-researcher, or starting a teacher-research group in your school? I know that you are laughing and scoffing, but stay with me. This is worthwhile. This can make a difference in your teaching life—a real difference that can benefit not only you but all those kids.
>
> You wouldn't need to have everyone in your group and yet everyone should be made to feel welcome. You should make it clear that you are not offering answers—actually you may only be offering more questions (now that should make everyone groan!). Have a couple of informal meetings (with food!) where people can experience a small sampling of what this might be about— teacher research can sound scary to people, so you want to keep things light and easy as people are sticking their toes in the water.

Brainstorm with your group some possible ideas, thoughts, or "mentionings" that people might be interested in exploring together. Talk a little about what people think the process might be like: Should we work as one large group? In pairs? All on the same question, individual questions, or a general theme?

People will begin to get the idea that this is not a "right answer" kind of thing but more a "let's do what suits us" kind of thing. Write it all down so people can look at this information again and think about where they might fit in.

As your meetings continue, I think you'll see a spirit of adventure develop, or maybe it's like being in a "risktakers club." People will begin to lay things on the line and say what they really think. Maybe they'll admit that they really believed something before, but as they ask questions, watch kids, take notes, and reflect on new information, their ideas are changing. That can be scary, so that's where the support needs to come in. Don't leave people out there on a limb all by themselves.

Talk about your own experiences; read and share professional books on the topic. Watch those kids some more. You'll begin to realize that conferences, books, videos, and experts are great (they are!), but you're the ones who can do authentic research that will clarify your thinking, answer some of your questions, and ultimately drive your work.

Good luck, have fun, and don't forget the food part.

Love,

Lois

Gail wrote to Mark Kenney, a first-year teacher whom she had mentored during his time as an instructional aide at Mapleton and whom she had taught in the fifth grade:

Dear Mark,

Congratulations on your new job teaching fifth grade in Bethel! They are fortunate to have you as part of their staff. I know that you will be a wonderful teacher. Since I was *your* fifth-grade teacher, I can't resist the temptation to continue sharing "words of wisdom" with you. When I think back on my first year of teaching, I remember it as a year of few answers and lots of questions, and at the time, I didn't see that as a good thing.

Like you, I was fortunate to have members of my family and friends to turn to when I was at my wit's end. Some of them even provided me with resources, bulletin board materials, and lesson plans. I didn't know it then, but the best resource I owned had been given to me by my college advisor, Dr. Ronald Dow. It wasn't a tangible resource, but it has remained with me throughout my teaching career.

Dr. Dow was never satisfied with an answer. He always followed it up with "Why?" Although his whys were usually directed toward answers I provided in English courses, he asked the same dreaded question in the methods courses he taught, and he added a few more. "Why did you choose that book? What do you expect your students to learn from it? How will you know they've learned it?" I couldn't escape his questions. They drove me crazy while, at the same time, I loved the challenge they provided. I would never have admitted it to Dr. Dow, but my greatest learning came from those questions.

Once my terror of being a first-year teacher subsided, Dr. Dow's love of questions helped me survive that first year of teaching. I eventually learned that my students were also intrigued and challenged by meaningful questions. I didn't question why this method was successful; I just knew it worked.

Unfortunately, it wasn't until many years later that I learned about the power of teacher inquiry as a classroom practice. I believe it is the most important resource we gave you at Mapleton Elementary School. Don't forget what you learned from our group. Teacher research provides concrete evidence of the ways that questions can improve classroom practices. Remember those many meetings when we struggled to figure out where spelling fit in our curriculum. (We were sometimes just as frustrated as you will be as a new teacher!) Remember the joy we felt while sharing student data in the teachers' room.

You may not be fortunate enough to have a teacher-research group in your school. Don't despair! You can turn to the writing of teacher-researchers to help you. You can always contact us by e-mail. And, most important of all, you can reflect on and question your own practice. Your students can help you find some answers. My hero Roland Barth says, "Powerful, replenishing learning comes to those who reflect on practice—and to those of us who are privy to their reflections." Use teacher research to replenish your teaching and to model for everyone who surrounds you.

Who knows? You might be someone's own special Dr. Dow.

Best wishes,

Gail

We offer you these examples hoping that you will feel included in the invitations they extend to teachers who might not yet consider themselves as researchers. Perhaps you'll be able to see yourself as a potential contributor to the kinds of conversations we've described, whether they happen with one or two colleagues in the teachers' room after school or on a larger scale. By becoming inquirers and basing our decisions on data we gather in response to our questions, all of us increase our chances of "pulling together" where spelling is concerned.

Recommended Resources

On Spelling in General

Bean, Wendy, and Chrys Bouffler. 1997. *Read, Write, Spell.* York, ME: Stenhouse.

Department for Education and Children's Services. 1997. *Spelling: From Beginnings to Independence.* Adelaide, South Australia: DECS.

Gillon, Jan. 1992. Dear Mrs. Gillon. In Judith Newman, ed., *Finding Our Own Way: Teachers Exploring Their Assumptions,* pp. 106–119. Portsmouth, NH: Heinemann.

Hughes, Margaret, and Dennis Searle. 1997. *The Violent E and Other Tricky Sounds: Learning to Spell from Kindergarten Through Grade 6.* York, ME: Stenhouse.

Laminack, Lester, and Katie Wood. 1996. *Spelling in Use: Looking Closely at Spelling in Whole-Language Classrooms.* Urbana, IL: National Council of Teachers of English.

National Council of Teachers of English. 1996. *Spelling: Taught or Caught?* [video]. Multimedia Center.

Rosencranz, Gladys. 1998. *The Spelling Book: Teaching Children How to Spell, Not What to Spell.* Newark, DE: International Reading Association.

Wilde, Sandra. 1992. *You Kan Red This: Spelling and Punctuation for Whole Language Classrooms.* Portsmouth, NH: Heinemann.

———, ed. 1996. Teaching Writers to Spell [Special issue]. *Primary Voices K–6* 4, 4.

———. 1997. *Ten Tough Questions About Spelling, Ten Tough Questions About Phonics* [cassette recording]. Portsmouth, NH: Heinemann.

On Teacher Research

Allen, JoBeth, Marilyn Cary, and Lisa Delgado. 1995. *Exploring Blue Highways: Literacy Reform, School Change, and the Creation of Learning Communities.* New York: Teachers College Press.

Anderson, Gary L., Kathryn Herr, and Ann Sigrid Nihlen. 1994. *Studying Your Own School: An Educator's Guide to Qualitative Practitioner Research.* Thousand Oaks, CA: Corwin.

Bisplinghoff, Betty Shockley, and JoBeth Allen. 1998. *Engaging Teachers: Creating Teaching and Researching Relationships.* Portsmouth, NH: Heinemann.

Bissex, Glenda. 1996. *Partial Truths: A Memoir and Essays on Reading, Writing, and Researching.* Portsmouth, NH: Heinemann.

Chandler, Kelly. 1997. Emergent Researchers: One Group's Beginnings. *Teacher Research: The Journal of Classroom Inquiry* 4, 2: 73–100.

Costa, Arthur. 1993. Through the Lens of a Critical Friend. *Educational Leadership* 51, 2: 49–51.

Ernst, Karen. 1994. A Community of Teachers Learning. *Teacher Research: The Journal of Classroom Inquiry* 1, 2: 63–74.

Goswami, Dixie, and Peter Stillman. 1987. *Reclaiming the Classroom: Teacher Research as an Agency for Change.* Portsmouth, NH: Boynton/Cook-Heinemann.

Hubbard, Ruth Shagoury, and Brenda Miller Power. 1993. *The Art of Classroom Inquiry: A Handbook for Teacher-Researchers.* Portsmouth, NH: Heinemann.

———. 1999. *Living the Questions: A Guide for Teacher-Researchers.* York, ME: Stenhouse.

Portalupi, JoAnn. 1993. Strategies for Working Toward a Research Question. *Teacher Research: The Journal of Classroom Inquiry* 1, 1: 58–63.

Power, Brenda Miller. 1996. *Taking Note: Improving Your Observational Notetaking.* York, ME: Stenhouse.

On Communicating with Parents

Crafton, Linda. 1994. *Challenges of Holistic Teaching: Answering the Tough Questions.* Norwood, MA: Christopher-Gordon.
This book is written in an accessible question-and-answer format. The brief section on invented spelling could be easily shared with parents.

Hughes, Margaret, and Dennis Searle. 1997. *The Violent E and Other Tricky Sounds: Learning to Spell from Kindergarten Through Grade 6.* York, ME: Stenhouse.
Chapter 10, "Commonly Asked Questions," discusses how parents can help teachers monitor students' known-word lists.

Laminack, Lester, and Katie Wood. 1996. *Spelling in Use: Looking Closely at Spelling in Whole-Language Classrooms.* Urbana, IL: National Council of Teachers of English.
Particularly useful is Chapter 5, "Communicating with Parents."

Phenix, Jo, and Doreen Scott-Dunne. 1994. *Spelling for Parents.* Markham, Ontario: Pembroke.
This brief book includes everything teachers could want parents to know about spelling. It's accessibly written, well organized, and remarkably inexpensive. Two lists are especially pithy: "How to Help Spelling Learning" and "How to Hinder Spelling Learning."

Power, Brenda Miller. 1999. *Parent Power: Energizing Home-School Communication.* Portsmouth, NH: Heinemann.
Part of the resource guide is a series of accessibly written newsletters that can be sent home to parents, including one on spelling.

Snowball, Diane, and Faye Bolton. 1999. *Spelling K–8: Planning and Teaching.* York, ME: Stenhouse.

Several chapters in the middle of the book close with excellent suggestions for parents who want to help their children with spelling at home.

Vopat, James. 1998. *More Than Bake Sales: The Resource Guide to Family Involvement in Education*. York, ME: Stenhouse.
Includes many reproducible items, as well as numerous examples of successful home-school collaboration and communication from a variety of schools.

On Spelling Assessment and Evaluation

Bean, Wendy, and Chrys Bouffler. 1997. *Read, Write, Spell*. York, ME: Stenhouse.
Chapter 5, "Assessment, Evaluation, and Reporting," includes a variety of useful checklists for students and teachers to use in evaluating spelling, as well as one for teachers to self-evaluate their spelling program.

Department for Education and Children's Services. 1997. *Spelling: From Beginnings to Independence*. Adelaide, South Australia: DECS.
In addition to the useful framework that undergirds Chapter 5, this book includes a description of the Writing Reading Assessment Program (WRAP), which can be used to evaluate student writing. It also has good suggestions on how to help students self-assess their spelling.

Rhodes, Lynn, and Nancy Shanklin. 1993. *Windows into Literacy*. Portsmouth, NH: Heinemann; and Lynne Rhodes. 1993. *Literacy Assessment: A Handbook of Instruments*. Portsmouth, NH: Heinemann.
These companion volumes include discussion of how to assess spelling within the context of writing, as well as a variety of checklists and other self-evaluation tools that are appropriate for a range of different grade levels.

Rosencranz, Gladys. 1998. *The Spelling Book: Teaching Children How to Spell, Not What to Spell*. Newark, DE: International Reading Association.
This book emphasizes a need for changing our focus from testing to gathering information that can direct future teaching and learning. In addition to numerous samples of spelling error analysis, it includes useful information about how to use dictation to see growth over time.

On Teacher-Research Grants

International Reading Association Teacher-Researcher Grants
PO Box 8139
Newark, DE 19714-8139
(302) 731-1600, ext. 226; www.reading.org
Grant applications for up to $5,000 are due in October.

National Council of English Teacher Researcher Program
NCTE Research Foundation
1111 W. Kenyon Road
Urbana, IL 61801-1096

(800) 369-6283; www.ncte.org
Grant applications for up to $5,000 are due in February.

Practitioner Research Communication and Mentoring Program
The Spencer Foundation
900 North Michigan Avenue, Suite 2800
Chicago, IL 60611-1542
(312) 337-7000; www.spencer.org
Grant applications for up to $15,000 are due in the fall and the spring.

If you are interested in obtaining a copy of our grant application for Spencer's
Practitioner Research Communication and Mentoring Program, please write to

Gail Gibson
Mapleton Elementary School
1642 Main Street
Mapleton, ME 04757
or send e-mail to gibsong@supt.sad1.k12.me.us.

Cover Letter

MAINE SCHOOL ADMINISTRATIVE DISTRICT NO. 1
Castle Hill - Chapman - Mapleton - Presque Isle - Westfield

Mapleton Elementary School

| 1642 Main Street | Mapleton, ME 04757 | 764-1589 |

Gail L. Gibson
Principal

May 22, 1998

Dear Parent or Guardian:

This year the staff at Mapleton Elementary School has been taking a look at our spelling instruction. In an effort to better understand how children learn to spell, we've been collecting samples of student writing, interviewing students about their strategies, and taking notes during classroom activities. We were recently awarded a grant from a national education foundation, and this summer we'll be spending a week together to discuss and analyze data we've collected throughout the year. We are planning to have a meeting in the fall to share what we've learned with parents and teachers from other schools; we have also been talking with an educational publisher about writing a book.

Recently, we realized that we were missing some very important information: the perspective of parents. We need your help. To assist us with our inquiry, please complete the enclosed *survey* and return it to school with one of your children by **Friday, May 29**. We will use this information to provide the best possible spelling program for our children.

We also need your permission to use student work samples in our writing and presentations. *Release forms* for each of your children are enclosed.

Thank you very much for your time. If you have any questions, please call me at school (764-1589).

Sincerely yours,

Gail Gibson

Gail Gibson, Principal

Spelling Questionnaire for Parents

1. How important do you feel spelling is? (circle one):
    not at all important   important   extremely important
    1   2   3   4   5
    Please explain: _____

2. How do you think children become good spellers? (Number the ways below, with the most important being #1, second most important being #2, and so on.)
    ___ reading
    ___ natural ability
    ___ workbook exercises
    ___ breaking words into syllables
    ___ memorization
    ___ studying words for tests
    ___ using a dictionary
    ___ writing
    ___ other _____

3a. What do you do at home to help your child or children be better spellers?

3b. Estimate how much time you spend per week helping each child with spelling.

4. What does your child do to figure out how to spell a word correctly? (Number the ways below, with the most frequent being #1, second most frequent being #2, and so on.)
    ___ ask someone for help
    ___ break it into smaller parts or syllables
    ___ look it up in the dictionary
    ___ use the spellchecker

___ use print from his or her environment (shirts, signs, labels)
___ find it in a book
___ write it several different ways and see what looks right
___ use a word he or she already knows how to spell
___ think about what it means
___ other _____

5. How much time do you think should be spent on spelling in school?
___ 20–30 minutes per day
___ 20–30 minutes per week
___ no specific time; it should be incorporated into writing time
___ other _____

6a. Please circle the statement with which you most agree:
a) Children should receive a separate grade on their report cards for spelling.
b) Spelling should be graded as a part of the writing process.

6b. If you believe that children should receive a separate grade for spelling, at what level should that grading begin? (circle one):
1 2 3 4 5 6 7 8 9 10 11 12

7a. Please circle the statement with which you most agree:
a) Spelling should be graded only in language arts.
b) Spelling should be graded in all content areas, such as science, math, and social studies.

7b. If you believe that children should be graded for spelling in the content areas, at what level should that grading begin? (circle one):
1 2 3 4 5 6 7 8 9 10 11 12

8. When is it important to spell correctly?
___ all the time
___ when work is going to be publicly displayed
___ homework assignments
___ journals
___ on tests
___ other _____

Check grade level(s) for your children:
K ____ 1 ____ 2 ____ 3 ____ 4 ____ 5 ____

Name _____ (optional)

Release Form

I, _____, give permission for the work, words, and descriptions of my child, _____, to be used in presentations and publications by teachers at Mapleton Elementary School and/or their research partner, Dr. Kelly Chandler.

I understand that inclusion of my child's work is strictly voluntary and that he/she may decide not to be included at any time. I understand that his or her real name will not be used in any publication or presentation.

___ Yes, I give permission.
___ No, I do not give permission.

_____
Signature of Parent/Guardian

_____
Date

_____
Mailing Address

_____
Telephone

Photo Release

I, _____, give permission for photographs taken in a school setting of my son/daughter, _____, to be used in publications or presentations by members of the faculty at Mapleton Elementary School and/or their research partner, Dr. Kelly Chandler.

____ Yes, I give permission.
____ No, I do not give permission.

_____

Signature of Parent/Guardian

_____

Date

Teacher-Research Retreat Schedule: Summer 1998

Basic Plan

7:30– 8:30 Breakfast
8:30–12:00 Work time (data analysis workshops, writing, discussion)
12:00– 1:00 Lunch
1:00– 1:30 Discussion of readings
1:30– 6:00 Independent time (people write, read, and meet to analyze data; they also have time to swim, take walks, and nap)
5:00 Time to get feedback on drafts (optional)
6:00– 7:00 Dinner
7:30– 8:30 Symposium planning (some nights)

Sunday, 6/28

Arrive at Libby's about noon; get settled in cabins; 4:00 start for meeting
Read-aloud: excerpt from introduction to *All That Matters* (Rief and Barbieri)
Freewrite: *Reflect on the year that has just passed. What stands out for you? What were some of its themes? memorable moments?* (writing for 10–15 minutes, then sharing around circle)
Chart ideas for book, then talk about ways everyone can contribute, other goals they have for the week
Read and discuss "Dear Mrs. Gillon"

Monday, 6/29

Read-aloud: *Regina's Big Mistake* (Moss)

Freewrite: *What effect has this year's focus on spelling had on your students? How do you know?*
Sharing freewrite in small groups, then debriefing in large group
Data workshop: parent surveys
Time to write or continue to analyze parent data after status check
Sharing time
Reading for discussion: "Seeing What Is Not Seen: Another Reason for Writing Up Teacher Research" (Hubbard)

Tuesday, 6/30

Read-aloud: "One Moment in Two Times" (Hankins)
Freewrite: *What have been your most lasting learnings about spelling this year?*
Data workshop: writing samples from schoolwide prompt
Readings for discussion: "Like a Chirping Bird" (Jones) and "Exploring Literature Through Student-Led Discussions" (Allen)
5:00: Time for feedback on writing (optional)

Wednesday, 7/1

Read-aloud: poems from *The Way It Is* (Stafford)
Freewrite: *What did you learn from analyzing data from the parent surveys?*
Data workshop: choice of data
No reading discussion
Evening: listen to Sandra Wilde tape, "Ten Tough Questions About Spelling," and discuss

Thursday, 7/2

Read-aloud: poems from *Carnival Evening* (Pastan)
Freewrite: *What advice do you have for other teachers—individuals and/or members of a group—who want to begin teacher research?*
Data workshop: choice of data
Reading for discussion: "A Little Too Little and a Lot Too Much"(Hubbard) and "Enlisting Students as Co-Researchers" (Hubbard)
5:00: time for feedback on writing (optional)

Friday, 7/3

Reflective writing and evaluation of the week before we leave at 9:30

References

Allen, JoBeth, Marilyn Cary, and Lisa Delgado. 1995. *Exploring Blue Highways: Literacy Reform, School Change, and the Creation of Learning Communities*. New York: Teachers College Press.

Atwell, Nancie. 1991. Wonderings to Pursue: The Writing Teacher as Researcher. In Brenda M. Power and Ruth S. Hubbard, eds., *Literacy in Process: The Heinemann Reader*, pp. 315–331. Portsmouth, NH: Heinemann.

Barth, Roland. 1995. Foreword. In Ronald Thorpe, ed., *The First Year as Principal: Real World Stories from America's Principals*. Portsmouth, NH: Heinemann.

Bean, Wendy, and Chrys Bouffler. 1997. *Read, Write, Spell*. York, ME: Stenhouse.

Bolton, Faye, and Diane Snowball. 1993a. *Ideas for Spelling*. Portsmouth, NH: Heinemann.

———. 1993b. *Teaching Spelling: A Practical Resource*. Portsmouth, NH: Heinemann.

Brooks, Jacqueline Grennon, and Martin G. Brooks. 1993. *In Search for Understanding: The Case for Constructivist Classrooms*. Alexandria, VA: Association for Supervision and Curriculum Development.

Brown, Ann, Bonnie Armbruster, and Linda Baker. 1986. The Role of Metacognition in Reading and Studying. In J. Orasanu, ed., *Reading Comprehension*, pp. 49–75. Hillsdale, NJ: Erlbaum.

Buchanan, Ethel. 1989. *Spelling in Whole Language Classrooms*. Winnipeg: Whole Language Consultants.

Button, Kathryn, Margaret Johnson, and Paige Furgerson. 1996. Interactive Writing in a Primary Classroom. *The Reading Teacher* 49, 6: 446–454.

Calkins, Lucy. 1983. *Lessons from a Child*. Portsmouth, NH: Heinemann.

———. 1986. *The Art of Teaching Writing*. Portsmouth, NH: Heinemann.

Campbell, Kimberly Hill. 1997a. Survival, Sustenance, and Making Sense: Journals as a Tool of the Trade. *Teacher Research: The Journal of Classroom Inquiry* 5, 1: 146–149.

———. 1997b. Celebrating "Conscious, Deliberate Thoughtfulness": An Interview with Deborah Meier. *Teacher Research: The Journal of Classroom Inquiry* 5, 1: 11–25.

Chomsky, Carol. 1970. Reading, Writing, and Phonology. *Harvard Educational Review* 40: 287–309.

Department for Education and Children's Services. 1997. *Spelling: From Beginnings to Independence*. Adelaide, South Australia: DECS.

Ehlert, Lois. 1990. *Growing Vegetable Soup*. New York: Harcourt Brace.

Fisher, Bobbi. 1995. *Thinking and Learning Together: Curriculum and Community in a Primary Classroom*. Portsmouth, NH: Heinemann.

Forest, Robert G., and Rebecca Sitton. 1998. *Quick-Word Handbook*. North Billerica, MA: Curriculum Associates.

Fountas, Irene, and Gay Su Pinnell. 1996. *Guided Reading: Good First Teaching for All Children*. Portsmouth, NH: Heinemann.

Gentry, J. Richard. 1982. An Analysis of Developmental Spelling in GNYS AT WRK. *The Reading Teacher* 36: 192–200.

———. 1997. *My Kid Can't Spell! Understanding and Assisting Your Child's Literacy Development*. Portsmouth, NH: Heinemann.

Glazer, Joan. 1998. Outstanding Educator in the Language Arts: Dorothy Strickland. *Language Arts* 76, 2: 164–170.

Goodman, Kenneth. 1986. *What's Whole in Whole Language?* Portsmouth, NH: Heinemann.

Goodman, Yetta. 1978. Kidwatching: An Alternative to Testing. *National Elementary School Principal* 57: 41–45.

Graves, Donald. 1983. *Writing: Teachers and Students at Work*. Portsmouth, NH: Heinemann.

Gwynne, Fred. 1976. *A Chocolate Moose for Dinner*. New York: Simon & Schuster.

Harvey, Stephanie. 1998. *Nonfiction Matters: Reading, Writing, and Research in Grades 3–8*. York, ME: Stenhouse.

Henderson, Edmund, and James W. Beers. 1980. *Developmental and Cognitive Aspects of Learning to Spell*. Newark, DE: International Reading Association.

Hubbard, Ruth. 1995. Making Sense of Teaching Tensions Through Writing. *Teacher Research: The Journal of Classroom Inquiry* 3, 1: 140–143.

Hubbard, Ruth Shagoury, and Brenda Miller Power. 1993. *The Art of Classroom Inquiry: A Handbook for Teacher-Researchers*. Portsmouth, NH: Heinemann.

Hughes, Margaret, and Dennis Searle. 1997. *The Violent E and Other Tricky Sounds: Learning to Spell from Kindergarten Through Grade 6*. York, ME: Stenhouse.

John-Steiner, Vera. 1985. *Notebooks of the Mind*. Albuquerque, NM: University of New Mexico Press.

Laminack, Lester, and Katie Wood. 1996. *Spelling in Use: Looking Closely at Spelling in Whole-Language Classrooms*. Urbana, IL: National Council of Teachers of English.

Meyer, Richard, Kim Larson, and Kim Zetterman. 1998. *Composing a Teacher Study Group: Learning About Inquiry in Primary Classrooms*. Mahwah, NJ: Erlbaum.

Mooney, Margaret. 1988. *Developing Life-Long Readers*. Wellington, NZ: Learning Media, Ministry of Education.

———. 1990. *Reading to, with, and by Children*. Katonah, NY: Richard C. Owen.

Portalupi, JoAnn. 1993. Strategies for Working Toward a Research Question. *Teacher Research: The Journal of Classroom Inquiry* 1, 1: 58–63.

Power, Brenda Miller. 1996. *Taking Note: Improving Your Observational Notetaking*. York, ME: Stenhouse.

Read, Charles. 1971. Pre-school Children's Knowledge of English Phonology. *Harvard Educational Review* 41: 1–34.

Rief, Linda, and Maureen Barbieri. 1994. *All That Matters: What Is It We Value in Schools and Beyond?* Portsmouth, NH: Heinemann.

Routman, Regie. 1994. *Invitations: Changing as Teachers and Learners, K–12.* Rev. ed. Portsmouth, NH: Heinemann.

Short, Kathy, Jerome Harste, with Carolyn Burke. 1996. *Creating Classrooms for Authors and Inquirers.* Portsmouth, NH: Heinemann.

Smith, Frank. 1985. *Reading Without Nonsense.* Second edition. New York: Teachers College Press.

———. 1988. Reading Like a Writer. In Frank Smith, ed., *Joining the Literacy Club,* pp. 17–31. Portsmouth, NH: Heinemann.

Smith, S. L., R. F. Carey, and Jerome Harste. 1982. The Contexts of Reading. In A. Berger and A. H. Robinson, eds., *Secondary School Reading,* pp. 21–38. Urbana, IL: ERIC Clearinghouse on Reading and Communication Skills.

Spinelli, Jerry. 1990. *Maniac Magee.* Boston: Little, Brown.

Stenmark, Jean Kerr, Virginia Thompson, and Ruth Cossey. 1986. *Family Math.* Berkeley, CA: The University of California.

Vygotsky, Lev. 1978. *Mind in Society: The Development of Higher Psychological Processes.* Cambridge, MA: MIT Press.

Wilde, Sandra. 1992. *You Kan Red This! Spelling and Punctuation for Whole Language Classrooms, K–6.* Portsmouth, NH: Heinemann.

———. 1996a. A Speller's Bill of Rights. *Primary Voices K–6* 4, 4: 7–10.

———, ed. 1996b. Teaching Writers to Spell [Special issue]. *Primary Voices K–6* 4, 4.

———. 1997. *Ten Tough Questions About Spelling, Ten Tough Questions About Phonics* [cassette recording]. Portsmouth, NH: Heinemann.

Wood, David. 1988. *How Children Think and Learn: The Social Contexts of Cognitive Development.* Cambridge, MA: Basil Blackwell.

Yarmouth [Maine] School Department. 1998. Yarmouth's Learning Results. http://www.yarmouth.k12.me.us/StratPlan/results.html